# BREAKING FREE FROM BIAS

# BREAKING FREE FROM BIAS

## Preventing Costly Complaints, Conflict and Talent Loss

**Marilyn O'Hearne, MA, MCC**

PNP Press • Kansas City, Missouri

# COPYRIGHT

**Breaking Free from Bias**

**PNP Press**

An imprint of Marilyn O'Hearne MSW MCC LLC
http://marilynoh.com



Cover Design: Susan Krupp

Published 2017

Library of Congress Control Number: 2017941732

ISBN-13: 978-0-9705122-0-8
ISBN-10: 0-9705122-0-1

# ADVANCE PRAISE FOR BREAKING FREE FROM BIAS

"Whether we choose to admit it or not, we all show up in life with our own biases. This is particularly true in the work environment. Bias can impact all of our decisions and can have a detrimental effect on a number of things including corporate culture, productivity, attraction and retention of top talent and profit to name a few. Marilyn's book *Breaking Free from Bias* can help you not only recognize your own biases and those you encounter, but provides some great strategies on how to overcome them and still realize the business success that you desire. I highly recommend adding this book to your collection!"

—Cal Misener, author of *The Freedom Framework*

"Marilyn O'Hearne has very special gifts. Once of them is that she epitomizes the concept of *Breaking Free from Bias* through her life story and unique experiences which bring so much depth to what she teaches and how she coaches people and organisations. *Breaking Free from Bias* is a must read for all HR leaders, politicians and those who are interested in expanding awareness on fair decision-making, choice-making and becoming a better human being."

—Darya Haitoglou, Psychologist & Systemic Relationship Coach (PCC), author of *Enrich Your Relationships*, former HR Talent Leader at Procter & Gamble Geneva HQ

"You don't know what you don't know. Unconscious bias can keep leaders from recognizing great talent and creating an engaging environment for a diverse employee population. This book helps leaders look in the mirror, discover personal bias and develop a plan to break free from these limiting patterns of thought."

—Bill Schwarz, Director Organizational Development, KCP&L

"Through *Breaking Free from Bias*, her coaching and her being, Marilyn O'Hearne contributes to the peace so needed today (as well as all people and organizations fulfilling their potential). As a United Nations worker committed to its values, this is a cause close to my heart."

—Yasser Saad, Head of National Office, Philippines, United Nations High Commissioner for Refugees

"Marilyn O'Hearne is the right person to learn from about bias. Her experience working with global organizations, teaching cross-cultural communication and coaching global leaders make her a knowledgeable expert in this area. Her book offers the Six Step Coaching IMPACT process as a powerful framework for all levels of organizations to increase the effectiveness of communication, conflict resolution, and risk management."

—Dr. Jane Alstatt, SPHR, PCC, Stakeholder Centered Coach, Adjunct Professor of School of Business, Park University

"This book is a 'must read' that demands attention with action! *Breaking Free from Bias* challenges each of us to examine the naked truth of who we are in our inner belief systems. The intricate details of our 'unconscious' affects every area of our lives including our jobs, education, relationships, community involvement, political choices and so much more."

—Dr. Evelyn Hill, author of *Women Under Construction*

"Marilyn brings compassion and pragmatic strategies for understanding our own biases and breaking free of them so that we might live a life of conscious choice. I highly recommend you buy this book and share it with your team. Over the past 20 years of coaching leaders and teams, I've come to appreciate how being unaware of our biases and how they impact our actions and decisions holds us back from developing authentic relationships."

—Cynder Niemela, MA, MBA, author, *Leading High Impact Teams: The Coach Approach to Peak Performance*

"Our decisions and opinions are often twisted by our biases. Whether we know it or not, these biases affect our quality of life, as individuals or as organizations. I recommend the six steps from Marilyn O'Hearne's *Breaking Free from Bias* as a great starting point for freeing the decision-making process from bias."

—Edward Mooney, Jr., Ed.D., author of "The Pearls of the Stone Man"

"This timely topic needs attention today, more than ever before! Over many years of ministry in the church and community I have observed how uninformed bias often becomes a prejudice communicated in favor of or against another person or group. I commend Marilyn on taking on this topic and offering a coaching model that can help improve ourselves and our community."

—Rev. Dr. Clayton L. Smith, Executive Pastor, Generosity and Stewardship, United Methodist Church of the Resurrection, co-author of *At the Crossroads: Leadership Lessons for the Second Half of Life*

"I share Marilyn O'Hearne's belief in our giftedness and the desire to pave the way for all, including organizations, to live up to their potential. Through examples and her 6-step process, she provides a clear path for Breaking Free from Bias to unleash potential and promote peace through decreased conflict."

—Pat Obuchowski, Founder of Gutsy Women Win and author of *Gutsy Women Win: How to Get Gutsy and Get Going*

"Marilyn O'Hearne combines her extensive executive coaching experience with insights about multi cultural competence–specifically our hidden biases and stereotypes. This is a timely and critical area, and Marilyn has shed light on this area with practical solutions. I found her easy to remember acronyms and concepts particularly powerful. For example, the 6-step process for leveraging our response to bias with greater IMPACT:

**I**dentifying bias

**M**anaging bias

**P**lan to unleash potential

**A**cting strategically with Awareness and Accountability

**C**ommunicating confidently

**T**aking stock and repeating successes

I wish Marilyn all the best for this book in the hope that it will have a strong and positive impact on reducing bias and stereotyping in the workplace."

—Debjani Biswas, President: Coachieve, LLC, Inclusion Catalyst, Author: 'Miserably Successful No More,' 'Unleash the Power of Diversity'

"We are aware of the implications of bias in our life. We understand getting free from bias results in more right and impactful decisions. Marilyn has beautifully explained this phenomena in her book Breaking Free from Bias. She has nicely illustrated through real life examples how to identify the biases and then work towards managing them for a more successful and better future."

—Dilep Misra, Founder DriveGrowth International: providing HR solutions, coaching, consulting and speaking

# DEDICATION

*For my parents, John O'Hearne, MD and Lillian O'Hearne, MD, shining examples of Breaking Free from Bias; for my daughters Amelia and Claire, who as a teacher and a pastor understand its urgent importance; for future generations, may they find this process easier and less necessary; and for our Creator who has uniquely gifted each of us.*

# CONTENTS

# PREFACE

Research shows increasing awareness about bias is not enough. *Breaking Free from Bias* offers six critical steps to implementtation and bottom line IMPACT. You can be part of the solution through identifying and managing biases and correcting their harmful effects, where everyone and every organization can live up their potential.

Each step has a chapter with organizational and sometimes personal examples, including IMPACT questions to guide you in your implementation.

The Introduction: What is bias? (hint: we all have it) Why is it so costly to you and your organization? How will you *break free from bias* through our approach? To discover your organization's level of bias, complete the Scorecard at the back of this book, or online at https://marilynoh.com/breaking-free-from-bias-scorecard.

Chapter 1: You hear about one of my clients' discovery of his own bias and how it was impacting his performance. I also reveal why I wrote the book, including my first encounters with bias. You are invited to reflect on your own story.

Chapter 2: Provides a deeper look into an organizational example of bias and the IMPACT of breaking free from bias.

Chapter 3: **Identifying Your Biases**: You are provided with three tools for identifying unconscious bias for yourself as well as your organization. Step One, the "**I**" in IMPACT.

Chapter 4: **Managing Your Bias So It Does Not Manage You!** You discover ways of managing your bias particularly as it relates to hiring and managing cultural differences. Step Two, the "**M**" in IMPACT.

Chapter 5: **Planning How to Unleash Potential**: Analysis of your situation with ACHE, my intercultural approach, then applying it to recruiting, developing and promoting talent including at the board level. A treasure hunt. ACHE stands for Awareness, Curiosity, Humility, Empathy. Step Three, the "**P**" in IMPACT.

Chapter 6: **Acting on Your Strategic Plan with Awareness and Accountability**: How to act strategically with awareness through feedback as well as building in accountability. You are also introduced to a model for challenging conversations. Step Four, the "**A**" in IMPACT.

Chapter 7: **Communicating Confidently about Bias to Reduce Costly Conflict**: How to obtain organizational buy-in for breaking free from bias, how to call out bias with care, what to listen for (including nonverbals) and how cultural communication differences can trigger bias (and what to do about it) are covered. Step Five, the "**C**" in IMPACT.

Chapter 8: **Taking Stock of Your Success and Repeating It**: Repeat the *Breaking Free from Bias* scorecard you took at the beginning to see your progress and what you want to continue. Step Six, the "T" in IMPACT.

Chapter 9 offers guidance about how to move forward with courage, persistence and partnership.

For *Breaking Free from Bias* updates and resources including your free toolkit, sign up at https://marilynoh.com/breaking-free-from-bias.

This book–and my programs–benefit from the contributions of clients and colleagues who have shared their unique personal experiences as well as given me feedback and challenged my perspectives. This is not an easy topic to confront alone, and the support of an experienced coach can elicit awareness and the completion of implementation steps that may not be possible on your own. Congratulations on your courage in choosing to become more aware of your own bias as well as that in your organization.

While I speak, write, coach and train on this big, deep topic, I am continually on the path to further awareness. Thank you for joining me.

# INTRODUCTION

***"What we hear and see through the filter of bias becomes our truth, while planting the seeds of conflict."***

–Charles F. Glassman, *Brain Drain: The Breakthrough That Will Change Your Life*

"Misaki is not speaking up in our team meetings," complains Joe in your leadership meeting. "With her lack of contribution, I am not sure our investment in her is paying off."

Pat is disappointed by Joe's remark. He considered his decision to hire the bright young woman from Japan to have been a *Breaking Free from Bias* move, and sees her as doing good work. Clearly Joe does not understand that Misaki was acting in the way she was culturally taught to be respectful: to wait until called on to speak and to defer to those with greater authority. Unaware of Misaki's cultural training, Joe unconsciously translated her not speaking up as failing to contribute.

Joe's *unconscious bias* plays out further when he chooses not to give her assignments in which she can develop and contribute and, ultimately, earn a promotion–all because he has labeled her as a non-contributor. Misaki is confused and hurt when despite her hard work she sees Joe giving choice assignments to as well as promoting others with less experience. Pat, a millennial who is also fairly new to the organization, sees Joe's bias but is unsure what to do about it given his rank. Without their organization's leadership implementing the six IMPACT steps in *Breaking Free from Bias*, Misaki might consider leaving–causing the organization to suffer the loss of her expertise, not to mention the cost of replacing her. If this occurs, Misaki, Joe, Pat, and the organization would all be hurt by the effects of bias. Pat also becomes a talent loss risk.

## What IS Bias?

First, what is *unconscious bias*? Bias is an inclination or prejudice in favor or against something, someone or a group, usually considered unfair. Unconscious or implicit bias happens out of our awareness. Neuroscience shows our brains are bombarded with up to 11 million bits of information and can only process 40 bits of information per moment (M. Zimmermann, *Neurophysiology of Sensory Systems*, as referred to in Google's Unconscious Bias Training). The remaining 10 million plus bits of information get unconsciously slotted into thousands of different categories, influenced by our background, cultural environment, and personal experience. This unconscious slotting forms *unconscious bias*. Thus unconscious bias happens automatically and is triggered by our brains making quick judgments and assessments of people and situations. *We all have unconscious bias.*

Because we *all* experience *unconscious bias*, there is no reason to experience shame. However, we each, as individuals and organizations, have a responsibility to identify and update our biases to prevent and correct their harmful effects. By doing so, we can create a more prosperous organization and peaceful world where everyone can fulfill their potential.

Joe's bias toward Misaki, stemming from his cultural background and his lack of understanding of hers, is an example of harmful unconscious bias. Other employees begin to notice a trend and complain that Joe is not promoting employees of different ethnicities. Trust plummets, affecting the culture and employee experience.

At Pat's professional organization meeting later that week, a colleague tells him, "Pat, I heard your organization is having a hard time recruiting and retaining young talent, especially women and people of different ethnicities." Ouch! Pat had heard of other millennial complaints of not being promoted quickly enough, but he had not realized his organization was taking on that reputation. *Unconscious bias* was now hampering talent recruitment and retention. Since Pat is involved in hiring and promotion decisions, he begins to fear for his job security, and he wonders how he can be a part of the solution. How will his organization grow and thrive if this continues?

## How Is Bias Impacting You and Your Organization?

Where do you see yourself in this scenario? Overwhelmed by complaints and conflict yourself? As a leader or human resources professional you spend 25 to 40 percent of your time managing complaints such as Joe's–conflict that can escalate to costly lawsuits. "In fact, 60-80 percent of all difficulties in organizations come from strained relationships among employees." (Zeynep Ilgaz, "Conflict Resolution: When Should Leaders Step In?" *Forbes,* May 15, 2014)

How can you get the rest of your work done under these circumstances? This takes its toll: on you, your position, your health, and your personal life, as well as on your entire organization. *Unconscious bias* is the unrecognized (because it is *unconscious*) root of much of this conflict and other organizational challenges that ripple out from it, which include the organizational culture, recruiting and retaining talent, and ensuring positive employee experience and engagement as people encounter bias barriers to living out their potential.

This is not how you envisioned life at your organization. Your mission is to be of service; you care about people, your organization, your career, your health. You want everyone, including yourself and the organization, to have the opportunity to live up to their full potential. You know that others achieving their potential will not take away from yours, but will contribute to your success and that of the organization.

You are not threatened, but you realize some employees are afraid they will lose their power if they share it with others.

Taken to an extreme, you have a bullying situation on your hands. Bullies operate from the stance that in order for them to be OK, to win, someone else must lose. No win/win. They tend to target people who they see as having less power or rank than themselves. Thus their targets can frequently be those who are not of the majority culture who are already negatively impacted by bias.

Even if you are not currently experiencing the pain of bias, you see it around you. Bias awareness training alone is not enough to get results, according to the most recent research. It must include implementation and empathy. Your empathy has revealed the painful effects of bias and the barriers it creates. And your empathy combined with action serves as a bridge to a more productive and peaceful workplace. Your empathy will build safety and acceptance, creating a barrier to us vs. them thinking while encouraging different perspectives. You are ready to not only learn more about it, but to take strategic steps to break free from bias for greater IMPACT.

This book's implementation approach is also grounded in empathy, not shaming. The intent is to open and continue the conversation about these issues while putting into action a proven process to break free from bias, an ongoing journey.

While anyone can benefit from the six *Breaking Free from Bias* IMPACT steps, this book is especially written for leaders and human resource professionals. What starts at the top of an organization will create the greatest impact.

## What Is the Big Deal About Bias?

By *Breaking Free from Bias*, you get to the root cause of conflict, reducing not only costly conflict, complaints and talent loss but also, particularly in the US, threats of lawsuits. This clears the path for success: yours, your co-workers, and the organization's. It is not only mission critical–your job depends on it. Our current changing global population and workplace demographics toward a more multicultural, global mix create more challenges that necessitate *Breaking Free from Bias*. From our opening example, you can see how bias could contribute to:

- loss of rising and mid-level talent;
- bullying and a hostile work environment;
- poor corporate reputation; and
- lawsuits for wrongful terminations and constructive dismissal, etc.

Some fear diversity will increase conflict and therefore decrease productivity, but the opposite is true.

Companies with greater diversity (gender, race, ethnicity) are up to 35 percent more profitable, according to McKinsey & Company's global "Diversity Matters" report, 2015. Their report confirms that diverse companies enjoy greater success winning top talent as well as improving customer orientation, employee satisfaction, and decision-making. In an article about the report, the authors write: "and all that leads to a virtuous cycle of increasing returns. This in turn suggests that other kinds of diversity–for example, in age, sexual orientation, and experience (such as a global mind-set and cultural fluency)–are also likely to bring some level of competitive advantage for (these) companies…" (Vivian Hunt, Dennis Layton, and Sara Prince, "Why Diversity Matters," January 2015)

"Wait a minute, why do I need this?" you may be thinking. You consider yourself and your organization multicultural and aware and see yourself as accepting or nonjudgmental. According to neuroscience, it is impossible for us to be free of *unconscious bias*, or judgment free, even with the best of intent. I invite you to stop and listen for the rumbling of *unconscious bias* and the echoing of its harmful effects within your organization, although you may not have recognized it as such. You will discover tools for this in the following chapters.

## How Will You Break Free from Bias?

Just as Pat and his leadership team learn to identify and manage *unconscious bias* in their organization through our coaching and training, this book will serve as your guide to identify and *break free from hidden bias* that *we all have* that results in conflict, and limits individual and thus organizational potential. Your mission of service, your stress level, your health, and your job depend on this.

The time is now. *Unconscious bias's* dangerous ripple effect is not going away. In fact, it is looming larger than ever. People are living in fear and pain, which affects their performance. While bias can start at an unconscious level, when it influences behavior, either unconsciously or consciously, that can result in discrimination, which can put you at risk for lawsuits and disrupts "social peace." "Social peace" or making sure people are being treated equitably is a term shared with me by a German colleague that is used in that country.

With my six step coach approach to the *Breaking Free from Bias* process in this book, I will partner with you as I have been partnering with other leaders and human resource professionals since 1998 so that you can Increase *your* IMPACT through:

**I**dentifying Your Unconscious Biases

**M**anaging Your Bias So It Does Not Manage You!

**P**lanning How to Unleash Potential

**A**cting on Your Strategic Plan with **A**wareness and **A**ccountability

**C**ommunicating Confidently about Bias to Reduce Costly Conflict

**T**aking Stock of Your Success and Repeating It

## The Results of Breaking Free from Bias

What are Pat and his team's results from implementing this six-step IMPACT *Breaking Free from Bias* process? First, they decrease costly conflict by 20 percent, improving the workplace culture and employee experience, resulting in 12 percent improvement in talent recruitment and retention (19 percent improvement cited in Corporate Executive Board, 2013). Second, all employees, including Pat, Misaki and Joe, recognize increased opportunities for potential, which in turn enhance the organization and ensure sustained success with talent recruitment and retention. Pat's stress level drops, and his health improves as he fulfills his mission of service and regains hope for his position and the organization.

You are invited to join me on a journey like Pat and his leadership team's in this book as we walk through the successful six-step IMPACT Coach Approach to the *Breaking Free from Bias* process applied to workplace examples. When you implement it with empathy, you and your leadership team can achieve the same enhanced results and success that Pat and his team now enjoy.

You can be the bias hero in your workplace: *breaking free from bias* for your own good, for the good of others and for the good of the organization. Be part of the solution, a shining light like my parents. This bias hero has been my image of you while writing this book. Even if you are too humble to embrace the hero image, you can make a positive impact. Together we can contribute to everyone and your organization living up to their potential while increasing peace in your workplace.

As you apply this six step IMPACT Coach Approach to the *Breaking Free from Bias* process, you and your colleagues will experience a more inclusive, thriving organization where *unconscious bias* is not being denied or forced underground in shame. Rather *unconscious bias* is humbly acknowledged, assumptions updated and intentional decisions and interactions rule. Your feeling of being overwhelmed decreases, and your career security increases.

## What Is the Coach Approach and ACHE?

What is the *Coach Approach* which I invite you to apply to the IMPACT process?

Increasing **a**wareness.

**C**urious, asking open, powerful questions that can challenge assumptions!

Demonstrating **h**umility, **e**mpathy and respect.

Providing a safe, supportive space for learning and development to take place.

Seeing each person (including yourself!) as creative, resourceful and whole, and building on individual and organizational strengths to fulfill potential.

Tapping into wisdom.

Listening deeply.

Exploring multiple perspectives.

The power of choosing your perspective and behavior.

Challenging assumptions.

Establishing clear measures for success.

Designing actions, goal setting, and managing progress with accountability.

Embedded within the coach approach is **ACHE**=**A**wareness, **C**uriosity, **H**umility and **E**mpathy. ACHE is my acronym and approach to intercultural work based on Janet Bennett's writings. Janet Bennett, Ph.D., is executive director of the Intercultural Communication Institute, an educator and writer. ACHE is also an example of my integration of cultural and coaching competencies. You will be learning more about its application in Chapters 5 and 7. "It is impossible to NOT work interculturally," I say, even in your own community when you consider all our different cultural identities. These include gender, ethnicity, age, native/non-native speaker, urban/rural, appearance, socio-economic level, education, sexual orientation, ability/disability, religion, etc.

Cultural identities are explored here for the purpose of understanding, not of stereotyping, and can vary due to our multiple cultural identities. Take Misaki, for example. If she had studied in the country she was working in, she might have already been breaking away from how she had been raised and learning to speak up more. Millennials globally are speaking up more, breaking free from previous cultural norms of deferring to those of higher rank and longer tenure.

The examples I use are real, although details have been changed to protect confidentiality, with some combining of stories to illustrate points. I am a pioneer in the integration of cultural and coaching competencies, training and mentoring coaches, leaders and human resource professionals in this approach. My experience spans work with clients and programs in 28 countries. I am one of approximately 782 Master Certified Coaches in the world.

Note: I receive articles on this topic daily and provide updates through my blog and newsletter. You may not find an example of every type of bias with every cultural variation. You *will* discover how to apply the successful six step IMPACT process to any situation to reduce costly conflict so that everyone lives up to their potential.

### *Invitation for IMPACT*

Before we go any further, I invite you to check in with yourself and your organization:

Go to my website, https://marilynoh.com/breaking-free-from-bias-scorecard, and use our *Breaking Free from Bias Scorecard* survey (part of the toolkit gift for signing up for updates and also found at the back of this book) to capture an image of where you and your organization are now to compare to where you are by the end of this book. This will aid you in establishing your development plan and benchmarking.

### *IMPACT Question*

Where do you see yourself and your organization currently on the *Breaking Free from Bias Scorecard?*

# CHAPTER 1 - WHAT YOU DO NOT KNOW *MAY* HURT YOU

## The Dangers of Unconscious Bias

***"Potential=Performance-Interference"***
–Tim Gallwey, author of *The Inner Game of Tennis*

### David's Surprise Discovery

My leadership coaching client David, a human resources leader, was referred to me because his 360 assessment scores did not match those of his peers or those above him. He did not accept their glowing feedback. We unearthed David's *unconscious bias* that was limiting both his impact and his mission of being of service and a positive change agent.

As a child, David had struggled with a speech impairment. He was teased when reading out loud and found it hard to communicate his thoughts in a way that others could easily understand. His bias was, "speech impairments limit capacity to make a meaningful contribution." Now, if you had asked David if he believed this about anyone else he would have said, "Of course not!"

His *unconscious bias* led to his belief: "They (the senior leaders) are not going to want to talk with me or hear what I have to say," which was holding him and his organization back.

Through their participation in my *Breaking Free from Bias* program combined with team coaching, David and his leadership team learned to increase their IMPACT through my six IMPACT step *Breaking Free from Bias* approach:

**I**dentify *unconscious biases* held about self and others through the Harvard Implicit Bias Assessment as well as my own and other tools which we put into play in-the-moment.

**M**anage their own and organizational biases by exercising their respectful curiosity and asking "Is this bias harmful? If so, what changes will we make?" and creating and beginning to implement an action plan.

**P**lan How to Unleash **P**otential. Their analysis revealed they were "fishing from the same pond" in their talent recruitment and promotion practices, which was also reflected in the "look alike" marketing images. The changes they implemented in these practices including an advocacy program which paved the way for all to reach their potential, including the organization and its profitability.

**A**ct on their Strategic Plan with **A**wareness and **A**ccountability. David's leadership team built in bias feedback and accountability in their strategic plan, calling out bias in a respectful way that keeps communication open.

Confidently Communicate about Bias to Reduce Costly Conflict, especially learning what to listen for that would signal bias was at play and develop a plan to manage it.

Take Stock of their Success and Repeat what is working well in order to reach full potential as well as avoid costly, unnecessary conflict. They scheduled this analysis quarterly.

The results? Each leadership team member as well as the organization was freed to reach their potential, and in the process, their culture and employee experience was enhanced, and conflict reduced by 20 percent by getting to this root cause. Talent recruitment and retention improved by 12 percent. David, his leadership team, and his organization enjoyed improved health and vitality with decreased stress. David was promoted as he updated his bias and beliefs and contributed more.

Of course, as in any coaching and bias work, the solutions were customized for David and his team. The IMPACT model is the distilled framework that you can quickly and easily begin to understand and implement for immediate results within your own context.

## Why I Created the Breaking Free from Bias Process

My vision is living and working in a world of shared power leading to peace and I feel called to contribute to peace through this work. Bias is a barrier to achieving that vision and at the root of much conflict, where leaders like you spend so much of your time. In this book you will find ways to cut through the root of much conflict, *unconscious bias*, nipping it in the bud so we can live and work in peace, and creating a culture and employee experience where everyone can reach their potential, enhancing organizational results. You fulfill your mission of service, of being a positive change agent.

Bias is an Interference in Tim Gallwey's equation that subtracts from performance to diminish potential. In addition to the business case, *unconscious bias* matters to me, and maybe to you, because of my passion about making the most of our resources. This reflects my value of stewardship and belief that people are our most valuable resource. This value and belief promote sustainability. I believe we are all connected and created to contribute through our unique gifts. An empathetic soul, I literally feel the pain when I hear the media stories of our not leveraging and utilizing everyone's unique gifts; losing out on opportunities and even lives due to *unconscious bias.*

In searching for solutions, I have read and viewed hundreds of articles and videos which have helped shape my process and programs. I continue to receive several articles a day, keeping up to date with the ever-expanding knowledge base.

This has enabled me to cut through all the information to the essence of what will truly free you and your organization to live out your mission and for all to reach their full potential.

## My Path to Greater Awareness

My bias journey, like some of yours, has been at times painful and discouraging. Bias is one of those topics where you see the word and say or think: "Not me!" Although so rewarding in terms of impact and results, it may be initially challenging to recognize your limiting *unconscious biases.* And experiencing others' harmful bias towards you can be extremely painful.

What got me started on exploring bias? I mentioned in the Introduction how *unconscious bias* forms, partially through our own experiences, culture and environment. I hesitate to share these stories because they hint of my age, and I fear the ageism bias!

Beginning at age five when I started school, I noticed how expectations were different for boys and girls. Learning to read, the stories were about Jane watching Dick do all of the activities, "Jane sees Dick run." These "reader" books, as well as female roles on TV, in movies, and in books helped perpetuate the bias that boys are active and girls are passive bystanders or in support roles. Thankfully this bias of women being in the background was counteracted by the example of my mom who was a doctor and an athlete. She also frequently told us we could be whatever we wanted to be. I have coached many rising female leaders to *break free* from this cultural bias to step into their leadership and influence, including taking credit for their work and negotiating their salaries. If I had not broken free from the cultural bias barrier toward women, you might not be reading this book.

By age nine, I had become painfully aware of additional cultural groups being perceived and treated differently, specifically Jews, African Americans, Japanese, and Russians. I found this confusing, unfair, and extremely upsetting. But certainly it was not as upsetting to me as it was to those on the receiving end of the bias. We had no African Americans in our school or neighborhood. One evening, however, my parents took us across town to an African American colleague's home for dinner. I was startled to see barbed wire fencing around their property and was frightened by their German Shepard dog barking and growling.

Ever curious, I asked the family, "Why do you have a barbed wire fence and a mean dog?"

"We fear for our safety in this neighborhood."

"Why don't you move to another neighborhood, like ours?"

"Because we are not allowed to live in your and other neighborhoods."

"Why?"

"Because of the color of our skin."

WHAT?! I continue to experience the shock and horror of that moment. Of discovering racial bias.

Today we still have racial, gender and other dividing lines in our communities and organizations based on *unconscious bias* which in some cases has grown into prejudice. These dividing lines limit potential and are at the heart of conflict. For example, women's earnings compared to men have barely improved since we explored career options in junior high school decades ago, and the number of Fortune 500 female leaders decreased last year. This can be a really discouraging realization. I still feel the pain especially related to how I have seen others experience bias, and now I can do more about it than I could as a child. You can, too. These bias-based community and organizational dividing lines are in sometimes violent conflict with the shifting of our world as it becomes more interconnected.

"Puta!" (whore) I was occasionally called in the streets of Madrid as a 20-year-old student, simply for looking like an American girl by wearing jeans, being lighter complected, and speaking with an accent–nothing to do with my behavior. Some Spaniards held this bias about American (US) girls traveling without a male family member. Men would try to also grab us. Spanish girls would not speak to us. "Ouch! Unfair!" I thought. This was one of my own "other side of the fence" experiences. I experienced quite a shock at this contrast from how I was viewed and treated in the US.

You do not have to leave your own city to experience bias. My first job out of graduate school was working in a community support organization where the director wanted me there. The majority of the families in that community were Italian-American and did not welcome me. The *unconscious bias* was "do not trust people who are not Italian-American." I am not

Italian-American. Finally, after many months, trust was built so that I could fulfill my role. The director helped by using her influence to advocate with the families to make use of my services.

Other experiences include not being initially chosen to co-lead a US bias training activity because I am white. I was chosen to coach United Nations leaders and then had to wait several years for a place to open due to a quota system. I have also experienced being one of only two Caucasian women in Kluang, Malaysia while teaching Organizational Behavior and International Business for Ottawa University. Children turned around to stare at me in restaurants. Although some of these experiences were painful at the time, I can be thankful to have experienced a little of what it is like to be viewed as the "other" so I can be more empathetic. That I still retained some privilege as a professor in Malaysia, a revered status in that culture, made that experience easier. In contrast, my lower rank status in Spain as a young American woman traveling on her own made that experience more challenging.

From interviewing people of color for my White Privilege Faculty Group and what I have heard throughout the years from coaching clients, program participants and colleagues, my experiences are only a tiny taste of their "other side of the fence" experiences. They frequently experience hiring, salary and promotion bias as well as micro-aggressions over their lifetimes. For example, Taneesha was told, "You are so articulate. You sound white." A micro aggression may seem to the sender to be a friendly comment but can reveal an underlying bias and be painful to the receiver. The implication was that sounding white was linked to being articulate and therefore sounding like someone of color was not.

Many examples exist of female leaders being mistaken as assistants when arriving at meetings. My mother, in her medical school interview, was accused of wanting to become a doctor just so she could find a husband. A gay colleague was questioned about his physical ability to handle construction work. I have heard recruiting teams express their uncertainty with how to address what accommodations might be necessary while interviewing people with disabilities. They need the information and do not want to offend. Military veterans sometimes face bias when re-entering the civilian workforce. With one organization, the CEO was biased in favor of hiring veterans, but there was not enough support given to the veterans in making the culture change to the organization. This resulted in costly talent loss.

## *Your IMPACT Story*

No matter which "side of the fence" you grew up on, wherever in this world, I invite you to:

Be still, take a few deep breaths.

Access some of your earliest memories about your own and others' cultural identities (ethnicities, gender, ability/disability, socio-economic level, age, gender, native/non-native speaker, and so forth).

Consider how you noticed your own and others' cultural identities impacting behaviors and opportunities.

For now, simply make a note of what comes up for you. We will come back to this in Chapter 3, where we will also explore ways to use storytelling organizationally. Remember we all have *unconscious bias.* The key is to break free from it one bias at a time, an ongoing journey.

# CHAPTER 2 - BREAKING FREE FROM BIAS FOR IMPACT

***"We must come to grips with our biases, or they will surely keep a grip on us."***

–Edward Mooney, Jr., Ed.D., author of "The Pearls of the Stone Man"

You find yourself spending so much of your time dealing with conflict, frustrated by its negative effects on your organization's culture, employee experience, and talent recruitment and retention. You are resourceful and have tried lots of solutions, but something keeps pulling people, and therefore the organization, off course, like a strong undercurrent. You may be fearing for your position, losing confidence, momentum, and motivation, and you know you are not the only one in your organization experiencing this. Have hope. Help is on the way!

Pat, the human resources leader you met in the Introduction, came for coaching for him and his leadership team. He was frustrated by how much time he was spending on conflict and talent recruitment and retention due to high turnover. Signs of employee disengagement spilling over to the organizational culture were pulling morale down. He had explored various interventions with minimum success and now was starting to feel concerned about the security of his own position. He was losing confidence.

Individual executive coaching had been successful for new and high potential leaders, and Pat realized at this time a broader, more systemic team approach was called for that would produce sustainable change. Pat knew of other leadership teams' sustainable change through coaching and his organization understood the return on investment as well as the importance of starting with the top level of leadership for the greatest impact.

As we (Pat, the leadership team, and I) explored beneath the surface, common biases against women, millennials, older workers, and workers of different ethnicities (among others) began to reveal themselves within the organization.

As objects that have been underwater for some time, some of these biases were smelly, slippery, and made a loud splash as they surfaced. Like barnacles attached to anchors, the surfacing biases sometimes carried with them anger, disappointment and lingering resentment, even pain. They were not "pretty" and Pat and the leadership team, like each of us, really did not want to recognize these biases as their own. They were reluctant and afraid to touch and handle these biases that had been lurking below the surface, creating the undercurrent of conflict and challenges with employee recruitment and retention.

Yet with success stories to point the way and steps you will be learning more about in this book, Pat and the leadership team began to not only identify these biases but to put processes and strategies into play to manage them.

Some of you may still be protesting, "Bias? Not me, not my organization!" The research shows the more confident you are, the greater the probability of bias.

What is *unconscious bias*? You learned in the Introduction that it is an automatic function of our brain–we all have it. The neuroscience behind *unconscious bias* shows our brains are bombarded with eleven million bits of information per moment, and they can only process forty bits of information per moment. Unconsciously (where we operate more than 98% of the time, according to neuroscientists such as Michael Gazzaniga, *The Mind's Past*, 2000) the other millions of bits of information are automatically slotted.

We like to think of ourselves as logical, rational decision makers (Kahneman's slow thinking, in the neocortex portion of our brain), and most of the time we are not. The unconscious is the fast part of what Daniel Kahneman describes in his *Thinking, Fast and Slow* book, 2011, centered in our evolutionary, primitive brain. The unconscious bias slotting especially occurs between like/dislike, safe/unsafe and approach/withdraw. This leads to us vs. them categories, biases, exclusion, conformity, homogeneity–regardless of our best intentions. For example, my family challenged my "they" statements referring to members of a political party which had gone from my disliking their ideas to seeing their ideas as unsafe, furthering the us vs. them political divide.

In another example, in Turkey, when people are "too much" of something not associated with their cultural identity, they end up slotted in the "ayip" or shameful category. For example, if a man is too soft or a woman too bold, it is "ayip." This encourages conformity. With increased awareness and training, people may begin to notice bias more but may be afraid or not know how to take action. This non-shaming approach to bias frees us and still carries responsibility for action steps you will learn more about.

A harmful (limiting) example from Pat's organization: a middle age white man is interviewing a young Hispanic female job candidate, Amelia, and makes a decision not to hire her due to the following *unconscious biases*:

> millennials do not stick around because they are only here to learn what they can and then will move on;
>
> she is likely to have or will have a family, which will make her less dedicated to and available for her job;
>
> Hispanic females do not contribute their ideas enough in leadership meetings.

We tend to hire people who are like us and/or align with our image of an ideal candidate, which can include ethnicity, gender, height and attractiveness. Even if hired, the employee who is not like us may not be promoted due to bias. When this happens, their unique contribution is limited rather than leveraged and leads to a premature, costly exit. In fact, many candidates do not make it to the interview stage because of *unconscious bias* regarding their cultural identities, which is why some organizations are now limiting cultural identity related information on resumes, including names. In 2015 then-UK prime minister David Cameron asked universities to implement anonymous "name-blind" applications to counteract unconscious bias towards people from a minority background, which is now under consideration. (*Raconteur,* October 2016). Chapter 4 includes more organizations' methods and success overcoming hiring bias.

What were Pat's organization's smelly, slippery biases that were the undercurrent contributing to conflict? Besides the bias mentioned in the hiring example toward a young, Hispanic woman, additional *unconscious bias* towards women was leading to complaints by female employees about how their male and female bosses were speaking to them, in ways they felt demeaned.

In another organization, it went so far that the boss's behavior was considered bullying, which led to loss of talent. A bully will target someone they harbor a bias against and consider to be "weaker." Frequently their targets are in an under represented, lower ranking group.

## IMPACT Means Business (Results)

What were Pat's organization's results of implementing the six step IMPACT *Breaking Free from Bias* process?

1. 12% increase in employee retention, which of course decreases the need for recruitment and training, positively affecting the bottom line

2. Increased recruitment of women and people of different ethnicities, generations, sexual orientation, ability/disability, etc., as their culture and reputation improved.

Pat experienced not only greater job security, but also joy and fulfillment in knowing he contributed to a more positive workplace experience and culture. These results made it more fun and peaceful to come to work not only for him, but for everyone in the organization, which boosted profits.

You are the frontline heroes of your organization-called to both serve the people (employees) and the organization itself. You want to experience, for yourself and others, a positive, peaceful, fun workplace experience and culture, where each person's contribution is valued, appreciated and leveraged. This leads to ease in talent recruitment and retention and decreased conflict, securing your position.

This book is written for you! You now have in your hands the work I am doing with others like Pat. You are invited to explore in this book how you can be a key player in identifying and managing the *unconscious bias* we all have. By so doing, you will reduce conflict, become better equipped to recruit and retain underrepresented cultural groups (multi-generations, women, ethnicities, etc.), and learn how diversity of perspectives also adds to the organizational culture, employee experience, profit and social peace.

In this book, you will discover how to implement the successful, manageable, immediately actionable six step process that turned around results for Pat and his leadership team. The next chapter starts with the first of the six steps, Identifying Your Unconscious Bias, both individually and organizationally. Step up into greater IMPACT as you and your organization *break free* from harmful biases we all have that can unknowingly be sabotaging success.

In the next six chapters you will learn how to **Increase your IMPACT through six steps:**

Identifying Your Unconscious Biases

Managing Your Bias So It Does Not Manage You!

Planning How to Unleash Potential

Acting on Your Strategic Plan with Awareness and Accountability

Communicating Confidently about Bias to Reduce Costly Conflict

Taking Stock of Your Success and Repeating It

# CHAPTER 3 - IDENTIFYING BIASES FOR INCREASED IMPACT

***"I Can See Clearly Now,"***
–Johnny Nash, Epic, 1972

*You are starting to see more clearly now.* You realize you and everyone else has *unconscious bias* and that we spend less than 2 percent of our time in our conscious mind. You want to learn how to make conscious decisions and help others do the same to ensure personal and organizational success. In this chapter you will learn to take the first steps toward seeing clearly, to move through the blinding clouds of bias we all experience, to success. This is the "I" in IMPACT: Identifying Bias.

Warning: identifying your unconscious bias can feel like you just conked your head on a doorway. It may be jarring, unfamiliar, and can even feel embarrassing. For others, when confronted with someone you have slotted in the danger section of your brain, you may be triggered to flee, fight, become defensive or agitated. For example, US police departments are providing unconscious bias training to their officers in response to the community outcries over the shootings of young African American men. Biased is not how we like to think of ourselves. Sometimes discovering our unconscious biases by collision can take a long time. In this chapter I will show you an easier, hopefully less painful, way.

First the story as promised in Chapter 1, which illustrates how early biases are formed and how they are identified. I have a photo from my birthday in Bali in 2014. Everyone looks happy and they are having fun. But it could have turned out much differently. When I was a child, my dad, a physician, took me and my three siblings to a meeting with visiting Russian physicians. At the time, they were Soviets and we had heard at school, through the media, and at church that the Soviets and Communism were a threat to be feared, that, like the "boogie man," they were "out to get us," to forcefully convert us. I did not consciously or intentionally choose to believe Soviets were scary, I was just bombarded with those messages.

We children were bored at the medical meeting, trying to stay relatively quiet, and playing the word game Hangman. Our quiet was interrupted by a Soviet physician asking what we were doing. We were startled by his speaking to us. We had not even noticed him approaching. After our explanation he showed concern, asking, "Isn't there some way you could play this game without killing someone?"

"Huh? I thought the Soviets were out to get us and scary. This man seems gentle, kind. He does not want to see anyone get hurt, even in a game," I wondered silently.

He did not fit with my image of Soviets. At first I felt confused. But surely my dad would not have taken us to this meeting if it had meant putting us in danger. I decided not all Soviets were scary. *This was my first experience of identifying and breaking free from my bias.*

Fast forward to a few years ago. I was in Bali helping with a coach training program with 23 Russian speaking colleagues. If I had not had this experience of identifying my bias toward Russians as a child and decided not all Russians were out to get me, my bias could still have been lurking in my brain and impaired the trust needed for us to work together productively. I have a photo from the training. I am seated in the center of a photo from the program with a big smile. We are all clapping. My colleagues are singing "Happy Birthday" to me in Russian. A birthday I will never forget and a wonderful reminder of the importance and impact of identifying bias at work.

Not only were my Russian colleagues trustworthy and kind, like my initial encounter with the Soviet physician; they were very affectionate and called me "sister." We were able to experience each other's warmth and, with the help of an interpreter, work towards understanding and appreciation of our cultures, contributing to a successful training program.

Just as in my childhood regarding Russians, we notice fears of different cultural groups being fanned to a dangerous level today. Of course you are concerned about the effects of those fears and their impact on your organization and its culture. *Breaking Free from Bias* is urgently needed now; a crucial ingredient to organizational success.

Google monitors how accepted their employees feel through surveys. From Google's re:Work, "Survey questions may touch on the following. 'Inclusion: Do female and male, under-represented minorities (URM) and non-URM, Googlers in each office location, feel equally included and valued?' Comparing responses to questions like 'I feel comfortable being myself at work, even when I am different from others,' and 'Google is a place where all types of Googlers (e.g., all genders, ethnicities, cultural backgrounds) can succeed to their full abilities' allow analysts to assess those feelings of inclusion. Google also focuses on the relationships employees have with their managers. Survey questions such as 'The actions of my manager show that he/she values the perspective I bring to the team, even if it is different from his/her own,' and 'My work group has a climate in which diverse perspectives are valued' help provide insight as well."

–re:Work with Google, https://reWork.withgoogle.com.

## Pausing and Centering

How do you move from the unconscious to the conscious to identify and begin to manage bias?

First, take a *pause*. In Chapter 1, I invited you to be still, take a few deep breaths, and access some of your earliest memories about your own and others' cultural identities. Then you noticed how cultural identities impact behaviors and opportunities for those of various ethnicities, genders, abilities/disabilities, socioeconomic levels, ages, native/non-native standings, etc. You made a note of what came up for you.

You just learned the first part of the first step of *identifying bias.* By pausing and taking a few deep breaths, according to neuroscience the blood flow shifts in our brain from the flooded amygdala, where we frequently operate out of fear and a sense of being overwhelmed, to the neocortex, where we are focused and conscious. This is called *centering* and provides a sense of being grounded, safe, and whole, as well as expanding available choices. If you need more than a few deep breaths to pause and make this shift, my video on Centering serves as a guide:

–https://marilynoh.com/.

Here is the script I use for the exercise:

*I invite you to sit or stand, with your feet firmly planted on the floor, and your bottom firmly planted in your chair if you are sitting.*

*Close your eyes and breathe deeply and slowly from your diaphragm.*

*I invite you to shift your body slightly to the left, experience that space, come back to center.*

*I invite you to shift your body slightly to the right, experience that space, and come back to center.*

*I invite you to shift your body slightly forward, experience that space, and come back to center.*

*As you shift your body slightly back, I invite you to imagine a great big fat dinosaur tail extended from the back of your body, and the tip of the tail is also in firm contact with the ground. Within that tail are all your strengths, gifts, and experiences that have brought you to this point in your life, and it will be with you as you move forward.*

*When you have experienced that, come back to center, open your eyes, and you may sit back down if you are standing.*

Doug Silsbee, who introduced me to a version of this centering exercise, says that if you practice it 10 times a day you will change your life. What you do by making this a frequent habit is bring more consciousness to your life, which will make it much easier to identify and manage your bias as well as sharpen your decision making. That is why mindfulness is so popular today. This centering pause "shifts us from a state of being triggered or responding automatically into being self-generating, resourceful, & creative." (Sillsbee, *Presence-Based Coaching*, p. 155)

My United Nations (UN) leadership coaching clients who, like many of you, work in fast paced, intercultural environments with a lot of responsibility on their shoulders, especially appreciate this process. My UN clients have successfully become aware of and managed their assumptions, such as generational entitlement or impatience with regional differences in the directness of communication.

## Methods of Identifying Bias

Now that your blood flow in your brain is where you can use it for conscious awareness, the next step is to identify your bias. I offer you three options for this step. First, I invite you to consider someone in your organization, especially someone towards whom you might be experiencing a negative reaction. I asked you to do this in Chapter 1, so you may already have someone in mind. Take a few deep breaths, center, and answer the questions in the image that follows.

As an example, the participants in Pat's leadership team paired up, paused, and considered all the assumptions they were making about the person across from them and then role-played an interview. One woman asked for clarification, "Are we assuming we already know each other?" Because, she added, if she had not already known the man she had been paired with, she would first need to determine if she was safe. All unknown men were slotted in the dangerous category. Imagine how that impacted trust and opportunities. And, in bringing her bias from her unconscious to her conscious, how it opened up new potential and possibilities.

Before you begin a conversation, look at these cultural identities and check out your unconscious bias:

1. What do I think I know about this person based on their cultural identities?
2. How could my assumptions get in the way?
3. What assumptions and biases do I need to update?
   (c) Marilyn O'Hearne MSW MCC LLC

Another participant in Pat's leadership team exercise noted, "When we meet people there is very little motivation for filtering out the negative observations since we are by nature programmed to protect ourselves and find safety in similarity." This is Kahneman's "slow thinking" and unconscious safety/unsafety slotting, referred to in Chapter 2, at work. This "slow thinking" or unconscious bias in the primitive brain worked well for protecting cavemen. Today it needs some updating, by shifting into the conscious or neocortex, or "slow thinking." You realize the impact of identifying those filters, those biases, so they are not managing you and your organization, the topic of our next chapter.

The second option is to take any of the 13 free Harvard Project Implicit Social Attitudes assessments:

–https://implicit.harvard.edu/implicit/selectatest.html.

When one of my coaching clients did she was surprised to discover her bias that women do not belong in STEM: (Science, Technology, Engineering, and Medicine) careers. This was not a conscious belief of hers. In fact, she is a leader in the medical field. If you had asked her she would have said, "Of course I believe women belong in STEM careers!" She has changed her behavior accordingly, increasing her awareness of how this bias impacts her hiring and promotion decisions within her department.

As a leader or human resource professional, your concerns might have been her bias rippling out to affect the culture and morale in her department, affecting conflict, talent recruitment and retention; or even ending up in complaints or a lawsuit. We are susceptible to biases even about our own gender, ethnicity, etc. Prepare yourself for unexpected results. This is the unconscious, after all!

The third option for identifying your bias is "listening to the system." This can be done through constellations work, deep democracy, or a series of story-based exercises. I introduce the first two as "read more" options for you below. I want you to have access to as many of the tools in my toolkit as possible. All three of these involve hearing from different parts and members of the organization, of the system. They also function to link the unconscious with the conscious in a powerful way to first identify and later manage bias.

Constellations: "Systemic coaching is a type of coaching that considers individuals, teams, and organizations in the context of the system in which they belong, rather than as isolated entities. It enables leaders and coaches to see patterns in their organizations, diagnose problems, identify areas lacking in resources, and make connections that might have gone unnoticed… Quickly identifying the roots of very challenging issues, providing a powerful diagnostic in individuals, teams and whole businesses." John Whittington, author of *System Coaching and Constellations*, 2016. –http://www.coachingconstellations.com/faqs/

Both constellations work and deep democracy have some roots in African culture and psychology and are practiced globally. Constellations draws from the Zulu culture and deep democracy "developed in the tension-ridden context of post-apartheid South Africa. The Lewis Method of Deep Democracy has been specifically customized to meet some of the most common challenges faced in any modern organizational and personal life… It is 'democratic' because it emphasizes that every voice matters and that decisions are wisest when majority and minority voices are both valued. It is 'deep' because it goes far beyond the engagement with ideas and instead surfaces emotions, intuitions, attachments, and identifies issues that make a conversation more honest and real." https://deep-democracy.net/

The series of *Inclusion Nudges* story based exercises can be summarized as follows:

"Reader theater": Half page employee stories (identifiers removed) are collected and then read by company employees and leaders. This results in empathy and insight into the small behaviors that "contribute to some people feeling excluded and others feeling included and valued by the company. The purpose is to highlight through personal stories the experience of exclusion and inclusion in the organisation and the impact this can have on the business; productivity, engagement, innovation, process improvement, company pride, talent retention and loyalty." This exercise was first developed by Hewlett Packard

GLEN (Gay & Lesbian Employees Network) Employee Resource Group, and then expanded to other diverse groups.

Display employees' real-life and personal experiences (with first person quotes) on a wall. The leaders read them and experience the pain of their colleagues, another empathy building exercise. "Also show the reverse business case (the loss) of not changing the current state... show findings from research illustrating how much each person underperforms (e.g., 30% decrease in decision-making ability) or how one person in a team experiencing harassment affects the productivity of the team." Then calculate how this translates into financial loss.

These examples come from the non-profit initiative The Global Inclusion Nudges Initiative and the Inclusion Nudges Guidebook. "The mission is to accelerate more inclusive workplaces, communities, societies, and make the world a greater place for everyone. Inclusion nudges are practical interventions designed based on behavioural insights to increase inclusion & equity in systems, processes, cultures, and behaviour in an easy & impactful way! The purpose of the initiative is to design, educate, collect, & share inclusion nudge examples from practitioners to practitioners worldwide to enable them to make changes for inclusion & equality in their sphere of influence. Visit the online action and community platform to learn more, get more examples, and share your examples."–http://inclusion-nudges.org

Congratulations on taking the first steps toward identifying and managing your and your organization's biases for personal and organizational success. In future chapters you will learn how to move into action, a crucial missing step in many bias awareness programs.

## *IMPACT Questions*

How might bias might be holding you back?

How (and how often) will you continue to practice the *pause* and identify your bias?

How is bias impacting your organization, the people you lead?

How will you start to lead others in identifying some of their *unconscious bias*?

How will you share this *identify* step with others in your organization?

# CHAPTER 4 - MANAGING BIAS SO IT DOES NOT MANAGE YOU

***"If you can't see past my name, you can't see me."***
–DaShanne Stokes, Civil Rights Thought Leader

You have seen the harmful results of bias in your organization, even bias towards the Human Resources Department–that it may be viewed as a tactical player rather than a valued, trusted contributor at the leadership level. You have discovered some of your own *unconscious bias*, dealt with the effects of biased hiring decisions, and seen how *unconscious bias* is the root cause of complaints and conflict that end up in your lap. It not only affects your work and the organization, it can be heartbreaking to see bias barriers preventing people, as well as your organization, from reaching their potential.

In this chapter we look at how to manage bias through determining whether bias is helping or harming, and how to "stretch with curiosity" as one way of managing bias for helpful rather than harmful results. We look at hiring bias, managing our own bias, as well as managing how cultural differences impact bias.

## Breaking Free from Hiring and Feedback Bias

One of my human resources partners described how predominately white and male his organization was when he was hired. Within six months he was not only invited to the leadership table, but also his hiring of outstanding young Hispanic women had prompted the organization to consider posting for jobs in the local Hispanic newspaper. Workplace culture began to shift, with less conflict, and better talent retention and recruitment.

All of this resulted in a bottom line lift, which contributed to his enduring and valued place at the leadership table. He broke free from bias twice. First, he broke free from bias against human resources professionals by moving beyond tactical expectations to leadership. Second, he broke free from a hiring bias against different ethnicities. Higher diversity means greater profit, as we have seen. This is partially due to expanding perspectives which leads to greater innovation.

Other companies are also experimenting with managing hiring bias. Deloitte UK is hiding the names of universities during the hiring process. This was after realizing that a bias existed towards hiring from certain universities. They also teamed up with the company, Rare, to incorporate a new screening process called "contextualisation" into their hiring process. Rare built an algorithm to highlight students who have overcome tough situations… which "allows us to look for potential, instead of always focusing on past performance. We are supporting social mobility and changing the way we recruit and support our people, to enhance the service we can provide to our clients and to make an impact that matters to our clients and to society," says Victoria Lawes, Head of UK Resourcing at Deloitte.

Pinterest implemented a Rooney Rule-type requirement where at least one person from an underrepresented background and one female candidate is interviewed for every open leadership position. This was to increase their hiring rate for full-time engineering roles to 30% female and to 8% male for people who are from "underrepresented ethnic backgrounds," and for non-engineering roles to 12% for people who are from underrepresented ethnic backgrounds. For every open position that becomes available within Facebook, at least one member of an underrepresented group must be interviewed. Walgreens made it their priority to hire disabled workers–which now account for 10% of their employees in their distribution centers. (Siofra Pratt,"6 Companies Doing Their Bit to Improve Diversity & Inclusion," socialtalent, October 5, 2016)

To keep the thinking fresh and innovative, team inclusion goals may also be set:

> "This was the team composition objective in Arla Foods, 2010-15.
>
> Max. 70% of team members with the same national/ethnic background
> Max. 70% of team members with the same gender
> Max. 70% of team members from the same generation
> Max. 70% of team members from the same educational/professional background"

This example comes from the non-profit initiative The Global Inclusion Nudges Initiative and the Inclusion Nudges Guidebook. "The mission is to accelerate more inclusive workplaces, communities, societies, and make the world a greater place for everyone! Inclusion nudges are practical interventions designed based on behavioural insights to increase inclusion & equity in systems, processes, cultures, and behaviour in an easy & impactful way! The purpose of the initiative is to design, educate, collect, & share inclusion nudge examples from practitioners to practitioners worldwide to enable them to make changes for inclusion & equality in their sphere of influence. Visit the online action and community platform to learn more, get more examples, and share your examples." –http://inclusion-nudges.org.

Hiring objectives such as this or a points system can curb hiring bias that may otherwise go unnoticed. A "close call" shared during one of my *Breaking Free from Bias* presentations that could have ended in a lawsuit occurred when the employees of one branch requested the candidate that scored 19 points lower on their competency based point system than the other candidate be hired. When asked why, the employees said they were concerned that the higher scoring candidate would not "fit in" based on others like them in their branch. When pressed further, the branch's young employees did not want to hire another midlife employee due to age bias. The organization's point system, designed to prevent such discrimination, prevailed and the higher scoring midlife employee was hired.

Of course, age bias can go the opposite way, against millennials. These biases can include beliefs that millennials are lazy, unpredictable, unreliable, unprofessional, and are resistant to workplace conduct rules. As seen with the hiring example of Amelia in Chapter 2, employers may fear millennials will not stay long enough to get a return on their investment.

"The common theme is a fear or a reluctance to hire people under 30, because they are unpredictable, and, 'they don't know how to work,'" says Cam Marston, author and founder of Generational Insights, a consulting firm that works with companies and employees on generational issues. "It's a life stage, not a character flaw," Scott Wooldridge concludes in "Millennials: The new victims of age discrimination?" (BenefitsPRO Magazine, September 30, 2015).

Giving frequent feedback rather than waiting for a yearly or semi-annual performance review works well for younger generations and avoids recency bias. With recency bias, only the most recent accomplishments or failures are remembered. Instant performance feedback systems can either be designed in-house or purchased from an external partner. These may also include an archive feature for a comprehensive review of performance.

## Cultural Differences Impacting Bias

"I want to know how to convince them of the truth, that they are wrong!" the leader told me in our initial coaching session, when I asked him to give me an example of his goals of improved negotiation and partnerships. Alarms sounded in my head. Knowing his client's culture tended toward more direct communication, I took a risk and said, "One of my favorite coaching questions is, 'Would you rather be right or in a relationship?'" and laughed. Thankfully, he laughed too, as he immediately became aware of the mismatch between his goals and his statement. Improved, sustainable negotiations do not result from insistence on being right.

I invited a shift in my Western European leadership coaching client's perspective, using the coach approach while maintaining a safe space to develop. Knowing he was working in South America, I asked about the cultural differences. Specifically I asked how direct he thought his communication was and how direct he thought his South American partners' communication was. This proved to be a big step in his *Breaking Free from Bias* that South Americans were "wrong" because of their indirect communication, which he saw as the cause for slow progress. In this case, I did not even use the word bias, but put the situation in the context of cultural differences in communication I thought the client could relate to. He learned to shift from trying to prove he was "right" to choosing where to adjust in order to make the most progress with his negotiating and external partnerships. "Attitude is almost everything," I say, and we are sometimes challenged to be aware of our own attitudes and bias.

At the conclusion of our coaching engagement, this client shared his additional learnings through our coaching: "Speak less, listen more, try to understand. View with the eyes of someone else:

asking 'what,' 'how' questions (modeled by his coach!). Like a game of chess." This client discovered through our coaching partnership how to implement these aspects of the coach approach integrated with the ACHE intercultural approach:

> Increasing **A**wareness: of the cultural differences in direct communication, resulting in labeling people of a different culture as "wrong."
>
> **C**urious, asking powerful questions that can challenge assumptions.
>
> Demonstrating **H**umility, **E**mpathy and respect: the client shifted from needing to prove he was "right" to humility, empathy and respect.
>
> Seeing each person (including yourself!) as creative, resourceful and whole, and building on individual and organizational strengths.
>
> Tapping into wisdom: "try to understand."
>
> Listening deeply: my listening inspired the client to listen more.
>
> Exploring multiple perspectives: "view with the eyes of someone else."

With a Western client who communicates directly I could pose a challenging question to start the process. However, with a less direct client who communicates more implicitly it can take longer to build trust, our relationship, and our agreement for how we will work together. We experience more of a flow, a sharing of intuition. "Like you are thinking my thoughts," my Japanese client reported. I would take care that my questions and statements would not result in a loss of face which could be experienced as embarrassing or insulting. Without an understanding and adjustment for cultural differences, I might be reinforcing a bias about "rude Westerners," and even lose the contract.

Remember Misaki from the introduction? Joe had labeled her as a non-contributor, not worth the organization's hiring investment, because he did not understand their cultural differences. She was operating out of her culture's practice of waiting until called on to speak, and especially after those with greater authority had spoken. Instead of labeling Misaki, Joe could have had an empathetic, humble, curious coach-like conversation with her to discover more about her culture including her approach to communicating in meetings.

Culture is the unique shared beliefs, values, communication and behavior of a community of interacting people. Recent research shows children begin to form bias based on parents' nonverbal as well as verbal messages from an early age. ("Exposure to Biased Nonverbal Signals Creates Social Biases in Preschool Children," *Psychological Science*, Vol 28, Issue 2, 2017, Skinner et al.) We can infer that organizational culture is impacted not only by written values and guidelines but also by its leaders' behavior which includes nonverbal communication such as eye contact and smiles, warmth or lack of, and how much time is spent with someone. We spend more time with people like us or of higher rank.

I begin programs and coaching by asking about participants' or clients' culture and how that is impacting them for the purpose of greater understanding. Participants and clients from other countries and "minority" cultural identities in my own country immediately respond. Those from the majority culture in the US may ask me what I mean. They sometimes view their culture as "the" culture and do not understand the question and this can take a little further exploring about the values and beliefs they absorbed from their culture.

Even during contracting for services this discussion about culture can save costly misunderstandings. As I was contracting with a Japanese company to provide executive coaching, I asked, "Do you want me to show up as my usual direct communicating Western self or adjust my communication to more indirect to align with your culture?" Their response: "We are an international company with offices in different countries including the US office. We want our leaders to be accustomed to direct communication, so please show up as your usual direct self."

Had I not asked that question and directly communicated with clients, and that was not what they wanted, I could have offended them and lost the contract. If I had assumed I should adjust my communication to less direct to align with their culture, I would not have been delivering what they wanted–why they hired a Western coach–and could have lost the contract. If I had asked a yes/no question rather than either/or, the polite response for them would have been yes, and I would not have discovered what they really wanted. Increased awareness of cultural differences and the assumptions and biases held towards those is crucial to business results.

This is not just true of Eastern and Western countries. Even within one country such as the US these same direct/indirect communication and other cultural differences exist, with Northeasterners generally perceived as the most direct, but this can also vary according to age, gender, ethnicity, profession, etc. Learning about cultural differences and adjusting when called for can be business and reputation saving. Taking these steps reduces the possibility of behavior furthering or confirming biases such as "rude Westerners" or "untrustworthy Easterners."

Yes, you are busy and may be wondering how you will carve out the time to have these kinds of conversations, and if you are up to the challenge. I have heard this concern before. What leaders discover is, like any new behavior, it can take time and practice to develop it, but once it is in place it saves you time you otherwise would have spent dealing with costly conflict and more. With your commitment to people and the organization achieving their potential, no one is better suited for this approach than you. You can get the support you need to achieve this. I am here for you.

Here are some intercultural tips my program participants and coaching clients find helpful:

Define what your intercultural communication will be. That can include where it is on the direct-to-indirect communication continuum. Note: your team declaring its communication will be respectful is not enough. Respect for Misaki may be waiting until the elders have spoken and she is called upon, while for Joe it may mean jumping in and contributing ideas as they relate to the conversation.

Humble curiosity = I am here to learn from you as a respected colleague. Questions begin with “help me understand” or “how” or “what,” without accusation or patronizing.

Frequent check-ins for understanding. During conversations where there are known cultural differences, especially in new relationships, stop and repeat back what you think you have understood and ask your conversational partners to do the same.

If you feel yourself getting pulled off track (clues: “how could he, she, they say that?!”):

Pause and take a few deep breaths.

> Focus on the shared vision or goal and look for agreement, as well for insight on how each can contribute.
>
> Brainstorm multiple perspectives and alternatives.
>
> Empathy: imagine what it is like from the other perspective.

## Managing My Own Bias

I found myself balking at a LinkedIn invitation to connect from someone whose photo showed them with a raised glass in a bar. "That does not look very professional," was the judgmental statement I heard myself think. As I paused to check in with myself, I discovered my own *unconscious bias* about people who spend time in bars. I asked myself what assumptions was I making about them? My assumptions were that people who spend time in bars tend to over-drink, which can get them into trouble. The trouble could include impaired driving, harm to their health, and to their relationships.

In updating my bias, I reminded myself that in Ireland the pub (bar) is the community center where people go to stay connected. As I tapped into my coaching curiosity and networked with a group that frequents bars locally, I learned that in my own community some people are using bars for the same reason (or, as with my Japanese clients, an extension of the office for networking), and it was not necessarily related to over-drinking or other negative associations I had held. If I had not updated this bias by using the steps below, I could have missed business networking opportunities and therefore limited my reach and impact. Within an organization, I might also have unconsciously avoided and even limited opportunities for known "bar people" by not giving them challenging assignments or not promoting them or advocating for their promotion, leading to negative effects on corporate culture, talent retention, complaints, etc.

In the next chapter I further address the importance of *Breaking Free from Bias* like this as you and your organization consider where and how to network in order to diversify your leadership to boost the bottom line.

**Two ways to Manage Your Bias**

1. **Once you have identified your Bias, ask yourself, is it helping or harming?** Example of helping: "When I spend time with positive people, I feel energized. So I choose to spend time with positive people." You may exercise an intentional bias in favor of underrepresented groups to increase diversity, as Pinterest and Deloitte did.

Example of harming: "_______ (fill in the blank with a cultural group, e.g., millennials, women, people of color) are not good employees or do not make good leaders because they are _______ (fill in the blank with, e.g., lazy, entitled, expect immediate success, etc.)"

What happens now? "If you can't see past my name, you can't see me," –DaShanne Stokes. Unless your organization is taking the names and other cultural identifiers off of resumes when considering who to call in for interviews, who to hire, and who to promote, bias leading to discriminatory hiring may be at play, with legal consequences in a worst case scenario. Other negative effects include the financial loss related to lack of diversity (referred to in the McKinsey *Diversity Matters* Report) as well as heartbreaking loss of potential, talent, and in some cases, costly organizational trust and reputation.

To be invited to the leadership table of course you need to demonstrate your value as a leader or human resources business consultant in ways that contribute to the Quadruple Bottom Line: People, Profit, Planet, and Purpose (a long-term, future orientation).

2. **Stretch yourself with curiosity:** Curiosity, and asking powerful questions, is a hallmark of the *coach approach.* If you discover your own bias against a certain religious group, for example, you could choose to attend their worship service, meeting, or an interfaith event, with an open mind, and curiosity, as I did when networking with people who hang out in bars. You choose your perspective: whether to look for positives or hold onto negative bias.

Research shows we are more likely to have less favorable reactions to those who are different from us. The practice of spending time with people who are different from us begins to shift this pattern when we are empathetic and curious. How could you address this within your organization? What could you plan to not only mix groups, or even departments, to stretch and manage bias? Consider the bias I mentioned toward the Human Resource Department, how engineering may view marketing, and vice versa, etc.

### How Stretching with Curiosity Leads to Greater Empathy, Respect and Results

One example of "stretching with curiosity" is a program where community members who were at odds with police interviewed each other and then did presentations based on their results which included speaking from the other's position, songs, role plays, etc. This resulted in greater respect, empathy, trust and reduced community conflict. I heard this on public radio, with community members who started by explaining their mistrust and ended with their sharing their greater understanding of the police officer's position. And vice versa. I even heard some lightness and playfulness after they interviewed each other, compared with their initial anger and resentment.

I do a "My Land, Your Land, Our Land" exercise with organizations to better understand what it is like to live in each other's "land." This can include experiencing what it is like in different departments, factions, or cultural groups, particularly effective during mergers and acquisitions and other times of organizational transition. This is again accomplished through asking questions, this time about what it is like in the other's "land" with additional experiential components. Greater awareness of what it is like to "walk in another's shoes" leads to greater collaboration, improved communication, and less conflict, producing better organizational results. By the end of the exercise, participants experience a sense of "Tear down this wall!" (US President Ronald Reagan to Soviet Premier Gorbachev.) Similar connections and insights for further action are achieved through the methods mentioned in Chapter 3:

systemic constellations work, deep democracy, and story-based exercises.

As part of a White Privilege Coach Faculty group, one of our assignments was to interview at least two whites and two people of color, asking only the question, "What does it mean to be white?" As a white, I felt really embarrassed to ask this question of people of color, fearing it might be offensive. All four that I interviewed turned out to be very ready to talk about it, which is not the norm according to YouTube videos I have seen on the topic. In the videos some interviewees had the same reaction as others do to the topic of bias, "Why are we still talking about this?"

The result of my interviews was a heightened awareness of how many "you are less than" messages people of color had received, from being barred from restrooms and restaurants, not promoted or at pay equity to not seeing anyone who looked like them on TV and in the movies when growing up and concluding they were not attractive because they did not look like the white stars. A demoralizing starting point. Understanding others' perspectives can result in increased empathy and support your *breaking free from bias.* This of course leads to organizational results, as we saw in my Western European client's example of working in South America.

### *IMPACT Questions*

How has your culture impacted how you see the world and colored your perceptions of others?

How do you want to stretch yourself and your organization with curiosity?

How will you spend more time with people who are different from you and promote this within your organization?

Congratulations on taking the first two steps toward greater IMPACT, influence, and income through **identifying and managing your Bias!**

# CHAPTER 5 - UNLEASHING POTENTIAL

## Searching for Buried Treasure

***"When I think about 'stretching myself with curiosity,' the image of stretching my neck to look over a tall wall comes to mind. I visualize a party happening on the other side of the wall, and I stretch myself to peek over the wall to check it out. I want to be part of it, and thus I stretch myself to find a way. Maybe that's one way to tap into our potential?"***

–Lawrence Andre, commenting on my blog at https://marilynoh.com

Yes, Lawrence, thanks for sharing your image of peeking over the wall to check out the party, stretching and finding a way to become part of it. I hope that is your experience of applying this book's crucial steps. I also imagine some on the "other side of the fence" wanting to join the party and feeling they are not welcome due to bias. Perhaps they feel they have stretched to the limit and even beyond. They are tired of being excluded. Once included, the other guests will delight in how they add to the party. In this chapter, we will look at how to access this untapped potential to enhance the organization and secure your career.

Let us dig deeper into bottom line boosting through searching for untapped potential treasure that has been buried by *unconscious bias.*

## Analysis with ACHE

I invite you, as I do the leadership teams and human resource professionals I work with, to:

Step into your ACHE (with an intent to increase **A**wareness, coach-like **C**uriosity in asking open questions, **H**umility and **E**mpathy). This means an understanding and appreciation of others' experiences and beliefs rather than clinging to the idea of being right.

Look around your organization and consider cultural identities (age, gender, ethnicity, etc.) You may want to refer back to the Chapter 3 image:

> What is the make-up of your board?
>
> Who makes up the leadership team?
>
> Who are your recent hires?
>
> Where and how are you seeking new talent?
>
> What is your organization's face to the world? (look at your marketing, media)
>
> Who is leaving your organization? (talent drain) Why? What is your process for discovering why?

Now that you have a clear picture of the cultural identities that you and your organization are recruiting, retaining, and promoting, consider:

> What treasure has been buried by bias?
>
> What cultural identities are missing, both within the organization and within its leadership?
>
> How is that helping or harming your organization?

And please note: as organizations continue to change, with new people stepping into leadership, this assessment needs to be repeated on a regular basis to check for bias. Remember, the Harvard Implicit Bias is a free assessment that can be used for this purpose, and there are additional assessments that give more of a team bias picture.

This analysis can be incredibly useful in finding "buried treasure." For example, we know organizations that have more women in leadership are more profitable. "A comprehensive global study that researched nearly 22,000 companies in 91 countries found businesses that include women in management experience more economic growth and are more profitable than companies where women are not in executive positions. The study, 'Is Gender Diversity Profitable? Evidence from a Global Study,' was conducted by The Peterson Institute for International Economics in conjunction with Ernst & Young (No. 3 on the 2016 DiversityInc Top 50 Companies for Diversity) and concluded that a company with even just 30 percent female leaders can contribute an additional 6 percentage points toward its net margin." Kaitlyn D'Onofrio, "Proof that Companies with More Women Executives Have Higher Profits," *DiversityInc.,* April 22, 2016. The study was from February 2016.

Yet according to research we spend more time talking with people who are like us and organizations tend to stay within their talent boxes. We know the damaging effects of that not only on profitability but also, related, on innovation. If everyone has the same perspective and experience, innovation, so necessary in our fast-paced world where the next new thing is quickly outdated, is stifled.

## "That Never Occurred to Me!"

I received a call urging me to send in my proxy vote for a company's annual shareholders' meeting for my retirement account. I said, "I do not want to vote because there are so few women on the board to vote for."

"You can propose someone," they responded. That had never occurred to me!

Let us explore that "never occurred to us" territory. At networking events I hear local leaders complaining there are not enough qualified "others" (non white males) to sit on their boards. The problem is not that there are not enough "others." The problem is that it never occurred to them *how* to look for diverse qualified candidates. They are fishing from the same pond they have always fished from and are not questioning why they keep catching the same fish.

How could you help with this? You have built trust in your organization. You do an analysis and initiate the hidden treasure conversation. Your stepping into leadership in this way not only secures your place at the leadership table but also accesses untapped potential and builds capacity. Making changes at the board and top leadership level have the biggest impact and also are probably the most challenging.

As mentioned in the last chapter with the successful young Hispanic women hires, sometimes you need to step out of the usual talent recruitment box or pond. How can you do that?

## From Analysis to Action

1. How did you answer the question, **"Where and how are you seeking new talent?"** Consider three additional ways you might do that, resulting in diverse fish which will add to the flavor of your organizational culture and enhance innovation and profit. In my recent interview for an article on diversifying boards for *CPA Insider*, I suggested seeking out networking events and people at those events who have different cultural identities. Try a Hispanic or African American Chamber of Commerce, for example, or university alumni groups whose members differ from your current board. To boost female participation, find a group like 2020 Women on Boards, a national campaign dedicated to increasing the percentage of women on corporate boards.

*Where and how are you networking?* Again, like is more comfortable with like and it takes breaking out of that to get to the new fish (reach new people). On a recent LinkedIn discussion I shared my networking approach of leaving each meeting with at least three new contacts (people I actually connected with, not just exchanged business cards with, of course). One man's honest response was that had "not occurred to" him, that he usually spent time catching up with the people he already knew at networking events.

This can be done in a fun way! In approaching a new conversational group, I sometimes playfully ask, "May I integrate this group?" especially if it is all male, or a different age than me. While this works for me as a mid-life Caucasian female in US professional meetings, its application may not be universal. I also approach individuals or groups who are in the minority in the room especially if they do not seem to know as many of the people. I sometimes also go to an empty table and see who shows up. You may want to partner with someone else at events to accomplish the goal of meeting three new people or even use these methods to seek new talent online. You can employ these methods even when networking with a specific goal in mind, such as wanting to meet someone with certain skills or positions.

2. How did you answer the question, **What is your organization's face to the world? (look at your marketing, media)** When the decision has been made to expand the diversity of your talent, I invite you to also consider whose photos are on your website, media, and marketing materials? That is your

organization's face to the world. If everyone looks the same, how will you attract and retain diverse talent? How will you, in a leadership or human resource consultative role, coordinate with other departments to ease and enhance talent recruitment and retention?

For example, Google's four minute unconscious bias video (YouTube) features women and men of different ethnicities, native and non-native speakers, from different departments, and with different abilities (examples: a self-described autistic engineer, a person with a guide dog). Google decided it would be to their (financial) benefit to go on a treasure hunt for untapped potential. They knew *unconscious bias* was responsible for burying and creating barriers for treasure/talent. Their *unconscious bias* training paid attention to how they painted the face of their organization in terms of who was featured in the training video. This not only helps with recruitment ("I see people who are like me") but also retention and client experience.

Some of Google's changes based on their breaking free from bias initiative as shown in the video include: 1. Realizing they had named all the meeting rooms after men and changing the names of some to include women. 2. Giving permission to call out bias when noticed. 3. Identifying and implementing bias breaking practices such as taking names off of resumes when hiring.

Also, "the Google Doodle images went from 23% representing women to 50% representing women after the discrepancy was discovered." https://reWork.withgoogle.com.The Google Doodle images are the ones that you see at the top of the Google internet page when you open a Google browser. And most of the artists were women.

3. **Once you have the diverse treasure, what do you do with them?**

Some organizations find success through instituting supported advocate programs. Just as fishing from the same pond for talent recruitment will not yield the desired results, the same is true for talent development, retention and promotion. My client Pat, from the introduction, overheard conversations about millennials not applying for positions because they did not see any being promoted. And a colleague told Pat at a professional meeting that he had heard "your organization is having a hard time recruiting and retaining young talent, especially women and people of different ethnicities."

In order to unleash potential and thus enhance their organization, Pat and his team identified some high potential employees within these cultural groups and developed an advocate approach to their promotion and retention.

In this advocate approach, the departmental leaders, instead of giving the choice assignments to and considering for promotions only "the usuals," intentionally gave some choice assignments to these identified high potentials of diverse cultural groups. In meetings regarding options for promotions, they spoke up (advocated) for these identified diverse high potentials.

My coaching and program included raising awareness for the leadership team of obstacles they might encounter and how to deal with them. For example, research shows that while men will go for higher positions even if they meet only a few of the criteria, women will only go for those positions when they feel they meet all the criteria. They might need extra encouragement, advocacy and coaching to go for positions where they do not meet 100% of the criteria. As noted earlier in the book, employees of different cultural groups may respond well to coaching which will encourage them to speak up more in meetings rather than waiting to be called on. Or to find alternative ways for them to be recognized as contributors.

For example, "Google's data showed that junior, female software engineers were not getting promoted at the same rate as their male counterparts." Their Analytics team discovered "men, who in many cultures are typically more comfortable self-promoting, were nominating themselves at higher rates than their equally qualified but, on average, less self-promoting female peers. To solve this, a respected senior leader shared the data with Googlers encouraging all engineers to self-nominate if they were ready, and told managers to keep their eyes open for promo-ready Googlers. Following the nudge, promotion rates equaled out." ("Unbiasing Guide: Gather data and measure decisions," re:Work with Google, https://reWork.withgoogle.com).

Gathering data and measuring decisions and outcomes is important to organizational success. "Employees' perceptions of people-decisions are as important as the actual outcomes of those decisions. To assess those perceptions, Google asks employees to share feedback on whether or not they believe the promotion process is fair, whether people are properly recognized for their contributions, and whether or not compensation is fair." ("Unbiasing Guide: Gather data and measure decisions," re:Work with Google, https://reWork.withgoogle.com)

When diverse talent see the advocate program in play, people like them being valued and promoted, their employee experience and hence attitude shifts with resulting talent retention and improved organizational reputation. The organizational culture becomes one of inclusion and hope for the future on both personal and organizational levels. We all know many organizations have written *breaking free from bias* values that reflect inclusion and respect but are not necessarily put into action until going through a process such as the one outlined in this chapter.

## *IMPACT Question*

Based on your analysis of your organization's buried talent and fishing practices, what potential unleashing actions will you take as a leader or human resource consultant to boost your organization's quadruple bottom line? (people, planet, profit, and purpose: future orientation for sustainability).

# CHAPTER 6 - ACTING ON YOUR STRATEGIC PLAN WITH AWARENESS AND ACCOUNTABILITY

## Acting Strategically

***"Anchor your IMPACT with Action, Awareness and Accountability."***

–Marilyn O'Hearne

The Coach Approach of building awareness and accountability as part of any development plan ensures ongoing impact. The awareness and mutual accountability provided through this approach increases the probability of sustainable success by up to 95% when you have an accountability partner (such as a coach), according to an ATD (Association for Talent Development) 2015 Accountability Study. We know a one time training or conversation will not produce the same results as ongoing awareness and accountability processes. Yet as a leader or human resource professional, especially in a small to mid-size organization, you do not always have the time for one on one follow up.

How will you build in accountability and awareness to ensure sustainable organizational success as you implement these IMPACT Bias steps?

First, you will increase awareness of *unconscious bias.* You will do this by helping leaders and employees recognize bias as an underlying cause of conflict, understand its effect on the organizational culture, and discover how to apply this awareness to retain and develop talent at minimum. You will accomplish this through sharing your own awareness and knowledge of *unconscious bias,* metrics and building in accountability. You may also consider what programs, which include accountability, to implement with your team and organization.

"Effective accountability programs draw from the budget, problem solving and communication systems. They emphasize performance measurement and review, team-based organizational structures and goals and positive discipline. Ideally, the accountability system is built by those who are enmeshed in it...We each promise to provide what others in the organization need to be effective in their jobs. Accountability monitors whether those promises are being kept and reminds us to hold up our end of the bargain. When we all keep our promises to each other the result is human reliability. And with human reliability, your organization can accomplish anything." Jon Thorne, "Accountability Is a System," *IndustryWeek,* February 23, 2016.

As an Awareness and Accountability example I introduce you to a young Hispanic woman "Ana." Her manager "John" was developing his leadership and therefore his department through our coaching. He was receiving feedback that others were disappointed in his hire of Ana, as she was seen as not contributing in meetings, like Misaki in a previous example.

Although John and Ana were of different ages, ethnicities and professional experience, John's awareness of cultural differences and bias increased through our coaching. Due to their trusted relationship and John's desire to see Ana succeed in their organization, John was able to have a caring conversation with Ana about how she was being perceived by others in the organization.

Ana realized John's intent in communicating with her was to help her succeed by increasing her awareness about the organizational cultural bias that "people who do not speak up in meetings are not contributors." Ana recognized her own belief, based on her upbringing, was that interrupting elders and those with greater authority is offensive and rude. Not only that, but risky.

Ana raised John's awareness by sharing the history of her parent's country of origin. In much of Latin America, those who spoke up lost their lives, first to Spanish conquerors and later to dictators. In some countries, reporters and those who speak out for a cause are still being killed. This fear sometimes carries over to the workplace with the belief, "If I speak up I might lose my job. I will wait to see if someone else says it." She had a choice: to update her bias, risk being passed over for promotions, or come up with a different alternative.

Ana chose to speak up more in meetings. She and John agreed he would continue to hold her accountable for doing so, conveying feedback in a way that would help her move forward with her career goals. Their Awareness and Accountability plan was based on their choices:

> John's wanting to provide opportunities for Ana to succeed and advance and
>
> Ana's willingness to receive feedback and decide which behaviors she wanted to change to increase her impact and influence.

This exemplifies a win/win/win. Ana wins because as she contributes more in meetings, her value to the organization becomes more recognized, increasing her impact and influence. She is now in a position to advance within the organization, promoting her career. John wins, because through Ana's increasing impact and influence, his department gains more recognition and itself becomes more productive as Ana's ideas are leveraged. The organization wins because it benefits not only from Ana's ideas but also John's department's increased productivity. The organizational culture and employee experience are also enhanced as additional workers of diverse cultural identities see Ana's ideas being recognized, valued, and put into action. This in turn enhances talent retention and recruitment.

Without my coaching and *Breaking Free from Bias* program, here is how their situation might have played out, with Ana and/or John's career derailing and/or the organization suffering:

> If John had not been aware of the impact of bias in this situation he might not have brought up the concern with

her, just believing what he was being told: that he had made a bad hire. This would have stifled her career and limited his department and the organization's impact. She may have resigned or been fired, both of which would be costly and could negatively influence talent retention, recruitment and organizational culture and reputation.

How did the coach approach with ACHE make the difference?

John and Ana had already established *trust*. They each knew the other had their best interest at heart, and that they could hold each other *accountable*.

They demonstrated *curiosity* about each others' culture. They increased their *awareness* of how cultural differences might be influencing leadership's perceptions about Ana's performance.

They *listened* to each other's perspectives.

*Humility*: neither took an "I am right, you are wrong" approach. I see the focus on self and being right as one of the biggest obstacles to breaking free from bias and leadership in general.

*Empathy*: they appreciated each other's position and took a "we" approach. They asked, "How can we work together for a win/win/win?"

The result: win/win/win–for the organization, Ana, and John. They even expanded the options for dealing with Ana's speaking up in meetings. The leadership could ask her questions during meetings, ask her to submit her comments in advance of meetings, and/or break into pairs during the meeting to encourage more participation.

You can claim these same results within your organization with the training and support of my *Breaking Free from Bias* program and with my further assistance as an external coach. Sometimes awareness and accountability within the organization are not enough! Leaders and potential leaders may need more individualized attention and coaching than the busy leader or human resource professional can provide. The following is another example.

A woman came to me for coaching for similar reasons as Ana's situation: not speaking up enough in meetings. However, "Jane" was a midlife white female raised in the rural Midwest of the US. She was rising up the leadership ladder. Her boss had communicated she needed to speak up more in meetings and could benefit from coaching. Our coaching revealed Jane's bias from her cultural upbringing that women should be in the background and therefore not front and center in meetings. She was being invited to step into her own power. Both she and her boss recognized she would benefit from one-on-one external coaching to make the awareness and behavioral shifts from long term patterns, with my accountability and support as well as her boss's.

In each coaching session the client reports on their follow through towards their development goals and decides how they will hold themselves accountable as well as how they want to be held accountable by their coach and any other accountability partners. When you follow through with your commitments, trust increases. Your trust in yourself as well as others' trust in you. The importance of leaders modeling this cannot be overestimated.

Jane and her organization reaped the results of our coaching. Her increased awareness and our additional accountability led to her stepping into her own power by speaking up, taking leadership of meetings, and delegating to others more. She also implemented a blend of Crucial, Fierce, and Nonviolent Conversation/Communication models in challenging conversations. She gradually let go of impossible perfectionism, focusing instead on excellence. These changes increased the organization's effectiveness and thus its productivity and profitability because Jane reduced the amount of time she was spending on conflicts, contributed more in meetings and kept her time and focus on her responsibilities. She also learned not to take on others' responsibilities as her own, such as rewriting her assistant's communications. "These sessions have helped me change who I am," she said.

## Challenging Conversations

My vision is shared power, leading to peace. Occasionally, as mentioned with bullies, there are individuals who are not willing to share power and seek to exercise power *over* others. This may be out of their awareness. In some cases, a person may be so invested in their project or area they have trouble relinquishing responsibility or turning it over to someone else. I coach my clients through a blend of the Crucial and Fierce Conversation models with Nonviolent Communication when this occurs. The conversation takes place one on one, because people who want to win at others' expense are usually very concerned about their image. Confronting them in front of others could be embarrassing, a loss of face. Remember the importance of humility and empathy.

You understand their position and your intent is not to convince them they are wrong. You do want to appeal to the other's self-interest and your desire to resolve the situation. When you frame the issue in terms of the effects of their behavior on their own reputation (how this appears to others) and organizational results, their motivation to change increases.

In Jane's case, her colleague Roberta was one of her greatest challenges in her new leadership role. Roberta had been in charge of an area that had become Jane's responsibility. In meetings Roberta consistently undermined Jane's leadership by interrupting her.

A conversation between Jane and Roberta might start like this:

Jane: "Roberta, thank you for meeting with me. I realize that you have been in charge of x project for years and have done well with it. A you know, our boss has asked me to take over x project as part of his shift to provide fresh perspectives and results. I want to talk about the effect of your behavior in our leadership meetings. When x project comes up, the team notices your taking the floor and interrupting me. When this happens, I feel disrespected. Other team members approach me and our boss in the hallway and express doubts about your ability to be a team player and accept change. The success of this and future projects relies on our finding a way to work through this. I want to resolve this situation, to ensure the success of x project, next quarter's results and to enjoy a positive working relationship with you. I want to hear your perspective. How can we have a good working relationship?"

Human resources and the leadership team serve as important support and resources, especially if the situation escalates. To learn more, read the Harvard Business Review article by Cheryl Dolan on Fierce Conversations:

http://blogs.hbr.org/cs/2010/04/are_bullies_in_your_work place.html

Marshall Rosenberg's Nonviolent Communication:

https://www.cnvc.org/Training/NVC-Concepts

and Crucial Conversations:

https://www.vitalsmarts.com/resource-center/

**Act on Your Strategic Plan with Awareness & Accountability (a two part step):**

This two-step process will help you to implement awareness and accountability within your strategic plan:

1. **Increase your awareness by asking for feedback.** Invite people to tell you what they hear you say and what they observe about your behavior. Based on their feedback, consider if your behavior reflects any *unconscious bias* and if so, what you want to change to increase your IMPACT. David, from Chapter 1, kept a notebook of others' feedback of him which helped update his self-limiting bias. How might you build this awareness into your meeting protocols and organizational practices?

2. **Increase your accountability with a partner:** Share with an accountability partner any of the steps you have already committed to take, such as *the pause*, asking yourself the "help or harm" question, "stretching yourself with curiosity," a change in your networking practices, etc. Invite your partner to share with you how he or she observes your following through. This accountability increases the likelihood of your success by up to 95%. How might you build this bias accountability into your team and organization with measurable results, including budget, problem solving and communication systems which emphasize review and goal integration?

Google's Four-Method plan for combatting *unconscious bias* includes their commitment to increased awareness and accountability. They encourage employees to call out bias when they see or hear it. "Evaluate Subtle Messages" and "Hold Everyone

Accountable" are part of their Four-Method plan, which includes asking for feedback.

As you have seen, **I**dentifying bias is the first IMPACT step, followed by **M**anaging bias and **A**cting strategically with Awareness and Accountability. Identifying bias is not enough. "The awareness of bias is part of the journey, but not the end, and it's the commitment to take action that makes all the difference," Sandra Kerr, Race Equality Director for Business in the Community. (Karen Higgenbottom, "Unconscious Bias Training Uncovers Discrimination," *Raconteur* October 31, 2016)

### *IMPACT Questions:*

How will you build accountability and awareness to ensure sustainable organizational success as you implement these IMPACT steps?

How are you implementing increased awareness of bias by asking others for feedback?

How are you sharing your awareness of others' bias through feedback?

How are you building in accountability for bias in your strategic plan?

How are you holding yourself accountable?

How are you holding others accountable?

# CHAPTER 7 - COMMUNICATING ABOUT BIAS TO REDUCE COSTLY CONFLICT

***"It ain't what you don't know that gets you into trouble. It's what you know for sure that just ain't so."***

–Josh Billings, 1874 US humorist (later attributed to Mark Twain)

How does Google do it? In the last chapter on Accountability and Awareness I referred to Google's 4 Method plan to combat *unconscious bias* which includes employees calling out bias when they see or hear it via "Evaluate Subtle Messages" and "Hold Everyone Accountable" programs which include asking for feedback. How do you call out bias when you see or hear it in a respectful, productive way? How do you get buy-in from the rest of the leadership team?

## Obtaining Buy-in for Breaking Free from Bias

It is one thing when a leader approaches you with the awareness of a bias related issue and wants your help in dealing with it. However, it is very different when you realize that bias related issues exist and you must summon the courage to have some challenging conversations with leaders that do not see it as a problem.

As with any initiative, it works best if you start at the top of the organization. In a recent initiative with an organization I have worked with, for example, the top leadership had six *unconscious bias* sessions over six weeks, and then all employees took a twenty-minute online training session. The top level of leadership spent the most time identifying and managing bias, realizing the entire organization would be observing their behavior and attitudes. How do you get this top tier buy-in?

Look at your organization's value statements, guiding principles, mission and/or vision statement. Usually there will be something related to respect or inclusion that you can tie your initiative to. Sharing the business case can also be helpful, as referenced throughout this book, especially in the introduction. "If companies want to prosper and retain their business advantage, they would benefit from having a diverse workforce, new McKinsey research finds. Of 366 public companies analyzed, those in the top quartile for racial and ethnic diversity are 35% more likely to have financial returns above national industry medians... Currently 97% of U.S. companies fail to have senior leadership teams that reflect the country's ethnic labor force... (which is) now over 56% non-white." (Ruchika Tulshyan, "Racially Diverse Companies Outperform Industry Norms by 35%", *Forbes,* 2015, referring to the 2015 McKinsey research)

You might also introduce one of the Identifying Bias exercises from Chapter 3 to increase awareness of underlying issues.

## Calling Out Bias with Care

Approaching workplace bias situations with care and ACHE: Awareness, Curiosity, Humility and Empathy contributes to effectiveness. We covered Awareness in the last chapter. Curiosity, addressed in Chapter 4, is a natural when using a coach approach as coaches ask questions to gain a better understanding. This can include questions like, "How do you want to be referred to, as Hispanic or Latina? Which would be more respectful?"

Humility is key in intercultural work. Given all our cultural identities along with the increasingly global nature of work, I see all work as intercultural. On the other hand, the quickest way to halt conversation and erode respect and trust is to come across as "My cultural perspective is right and yours is wrong." Can you be confident and humble at the same time? Yes, yet some suggest the more confident we are in our position, the higher likelihood of bias. Also, research has shown that attaining higher socioeconomic status, which usually comes with leadership, diminishes empathy, where it is needed. (Michael W. Kraus, Stéphane Côté, Dacher Keltner, *Psychological Science,* October 10, 2010)

Empathy is "the ability to share someone else's feelings or experiences by imagining what it would be like to be in that person's situation" (Cambridge Dictionary) and is a hallmark of both emotional and cultural intelligence. Some studies referenced on the following website also show that empathy can improve leadership ability and facilitate effective communication. Want to check your and your team's empathy level? Take the quiz:

–http://greatergood.berkeley.edu/quizzes/take_quiz/14.

That site also contains tips for further developing empathy, which include cultivating curiosity, imagining what it is like to be "in another's shoes," and the centering or mindfulness you experienced in Chapter 3.

One human resource leader and university adjunct professor, Randy Woehl, when he hears a statement that reflects bias, has learned to invite the person to repeat what they have just said and substitute their own name, race, etc. He follows this with, "Something's happened in your life that you've lumped everyone together." Hear the IMPACT steps here? 1. identifying the bias, 2. an exercise to *Break Free from Bias*, 3. stimulate awareness by providing feedback through 4. communication.

An example would be the blanket statement, "Women (or human resource professionals) are not business minded, so why invite them to the leadership table?" The next step would be, if the speaker is male, to substitute the word "men" for "women" or "human resource professionals." And then explore how to further update or break free from the bias so it is not sabotaging organizational success, building in the awareness and accountability from Step 4 in the last chapter. Of course, you will want to have these sensitive conversations one on one to avoid embarrassment or humiliation and to frame it in a way that relates to organizational effectiveness and career success.

Example: Randy's exercise could be followed with, "When you lump all women together and say they are not business minded and therefore do not belong at the leadership table, you actually limit the profitability of our organization, as research shows women in leadership positions boost the bottom line. We need diverse perspectives to continue to innovate and keep our leading edge. And you also expose our organization to costly complaints, conflict, and talent loss which can ripple out into challenges with employee engagement, talent recruitment and retention. I have been remiss in not addressing this with you earlier. I want to resolve this." This is another example of the Crucial/Fierce/Nonviolent Conversation process. "When you do ____, this is the result ____ (how it affects me, our organization)." You would then recognize your part in the issue and state your desire to resolve it. Do not forget the importance of humility, empathy, and intent. Your intent is to partner with them in improving the situation, not to prove them wrong, and that includes understanding their perspective.

As stated previously, generation and time spent in other cultures may impact the level of directness and who speaks up. A Latin American colleague reports that millennials speak up more, especially those in the middle or upper class, whose parents kept them "in a bubble." These millennials have not experienced the fear of living under a dictatorship as their parents did. Their parents have protected their children from the harsh and fearful realities they faced growing up. Others may fear that by speaking up about bias they will be seen as a troublemaker or lose their job.

## What to Listen For

In Chapter 5 we asked a lot of questions regarding looking for buried treasure, or untapped potential, especially looking at talent recruitment, retention, promotion, and leadership. Now it is time to dig a little deeper. Besides catching blanket bias statements, consider these scenarios which frequently lead to unnecessary conflict when not addressed (these all require deep listening, a key factor in the coach approach):

**Who are people talking with or not talking with?** Example: men only communicating with men instead of female co-workers because their bias is "women should not be in the workplace." Women were noticing it and complaining about this practice and the workflow was interrupted as the men bypassed the women.

**How are people talking with each other?** Sometimes how men communicate with each other is considered disrespectful by their female co-workers, or again generational differences. The use of swear words or cursing is one example. Also, tone of voice, nonverbals are so important. Do you hear respect or condescension toward certain cultural groups which may reflect and perpetuate *unconscious bias*?

What do you notice employees posting on social media, or in emails that may reflect bias, and how do you handle that? Do you have a company policy about it?

**How is communication received when it comes from certain cultural groups**? For example, when a male is heard communicating directly, that may be received as "normal." When a white woman is communicating directly, that may be received as "b____y." A direct black woman? "Angry b____."

"In one study, where a total of 248 reviews from 180 people were collected, 58.9% of reviews for men contained critical feedback compared with 87.9% of the reviews received by women. And though men and women were both given constructive feedback, women received feedback that also included suggestions to 'pipe down.' The feedback included observed personal traits as coming off too aggressive, abrasive, watching their tone, taking a step back to let others shine, and to be less judgmental. Another study conducted by Yale University found that others, especially those in power, view women who talked a lot negatively, finding them 'domineering and controlling,' and consequently less suitable for leadership positions than men who spoke the same amount." (Christine Rho, "How Does Gender Bias Really Affect Women in the Workplace?" Modern Workforce by Everwise, March 24, 2016)

Also, direct communication by any Westerner (US, Europe) with an Easterner (Japanese, Korean, Thai, Indonesian) may be considered rude, while an Easterner's indirect communication may be received with impatience or perceived as not contributing by Westerners. Consider the complaints people bring you and the "parking lot" or "hallway" conversations after meetings and determine what might be related to bias.

## Cultural Communication Differences Can Trigger Bias

I offer the following examples of nonverbal communication as well as the importance of curiosity and awareness. Before I left for Malaysia and Hong Kong to teach International Business as well as Organizational Behavior for a US University, I was advised that the students would not be accustomed to speaking in class without being called on. As faculty, I was instructed to encourage and give students permission to participate in class discussions (expecting the students to adjust to US classroom culture, illustrating the first part of the step, below), and also to make use of small group learning.

Imagine how surprised I would have been if I had not been aware of this cultural difference and been unprepared for students not speaking up in class. When these surprises occur, misunderstandings or even negative attribution can follow. For example, a professor surprised by students not speaking up might conclude: 1. their students were not understanding them or 2. their students were not prepared for class and therefore could not participate in the discussion (further concluding "they are lazy" or some other negative assumption related to their *unconscious bias*).

There was a lot I was *not* told about what to expect regarding cultural differences. If I had not exercised my curiosity and done the research myself, it could have been disastrous.

Example: a fellow Adjunct Professor I interviewed had made eye contact with all her students. A Muslim male Malay interpreted this as romantic interest and sent her flowers and proposed marriage. She was already married and unprepared for this situation. I was thankful I took the time to do the research regarding nonverbal communication, which also included discovering not to pass out papers using what Malays consider the "dirty hand." If I had not discovered the latter and passed out papers with my "dirty hand," this behavior could have triggered my students' bias of me as disrespectful and diminished my effectiveness.

## 2 Part Step to Confidently Communicating about Bias

Start with an awareness and understanding of your own culture and biases. Next, curiously consider the culture of those you are communicating with, and decide how you can most effectively communicate together to make meaning of shared experiences. This can include acknowledging the cultural communication differences of different team or department members and what type of culture and communication that group chooses together that will work best. This can also be applied to virtual teams. Humility comes into play in remembering your way or perspective is not "right" and others' "wrong," but on different points of the spectrum and in choosing what works best.

When you consider communication, include nonverbal communication and cultural norms. Gestures carry different meanings, as does silence, formality, how directly you communicate and the pacing (how rapidly you speak), etc. In the US, East coast speakers are known for speaking more directly and rapidly than those in the Midwest or South, for example. Western Europeans and North Americans are generally considered more direct than those in the Southern Hemisphere and in the East, although there is variance according to generation, time spent in and with other cultures, introvert/extrovert, etc. Remember the examples of women acculturated to not speaking up and how that was effecting their reaching their potential within the organization and different perceptions of direct communication based on culture.

**Bonus tip for leaders:** Making cultural adjustments to leverage the contributions of diverse groups contributes to innovation and avoiding group-think. In Malaysia and with global teams, that has involved making use of small group rather than whole group discussions resulting in greater contributions from those who would usually defer in large groups. Women and other cultural identities who are acculturated to defer in group discussions could contribute more when asked to contribute in writing, in pairs, and when called on.

## *IMPACT Questions*

How are you listening for and challenging bias with care when you hear it?

How are you getting buy-in for *Breaking Free from Bias* programs and coaching, especially when the need may not be seen by the top-level leadership?

How are you considering nonverbal communication and cultural differences?

# CHAPTER 8 - TAKE STOCK OF YOUR SUCCESS AND REPEAT

***"Pausing + IMPACT steps = successfully breaking free from bias."***

–Marilyn O'Hearne

The final IMPACT Step is: Take Stock of Your Success and Repeat:

How are you doing with the six steps to increase your IMPACT? Now is the time to review the progress you and your organization are making, based on your working through the six steps and the data you have been collecting around the results. This is the Breaking Free from Bias Scorecard you downloaded from https://marilynoh.com/breaking-free-from-bias-scorecard or accessed in the back of this book and completed when you read the introduction. By completing your scorecard for the second time and comparing the two, you will see what was successful and choose to continue those actions for continued success.

For example, in my coaching session this morning with a United Nations leader, my client repeated his success with taking a centering pause, our first IMPACT step to *breaking free from bias.* In this session my client was practicing a pause before a performance conversation with an employee in order to prevent bias from impacting his feedback for the employee. Remembering to take time to pause, a step you learned in Chapter 3 to Identify Bias, is an example of Taking Stock of Your Success and Repeat, the final IMPACT step. Talk about a fast paced, high pressure work environment in the UN! **If they can do it, you can, too.**

These leaders are "on the ground" in world "hot spots." In a world where we are bombarded with information (11 million bits/moment, while our brains can process only 40 bits/moment) and operate 98 percent of the time out of the unconscious, I invite you to *pause,* as well as practice the additional five steps. Again, the pause is where you consider your bias before communicating. Pausing is crucial to *Breaking Free from Bias* to increase your IMPACT because it brings you into your conscious where you can make less biased decisions.

"One second can be the difference between achieving desired results or not. One second is all it takes to become less reactive and more in tune with the moment. In that one second lies the opportunity to improve the way you decide and direct, the way you engage and lead. That's an enormous advantage for leaders in fast-paced, high-pressure jobs." Rasmus Hougaard, Jacqueline Carter and Gitte Dybkjaer," Spending 10 Minutes a Day on Mindfulness Subtly Changes the Way You React to Everything," *Harvard Business Review,* January 17, 2017. The centering you learned in Chapter 3 is a type of mindfulness activity.

"Pausing + IMPACT steps = successfully breaking free from bias." Keep in mind this is an ongoing process.

I invite you to reflect on your learning journey so far and your progress on:

**Identifying your biases (Pause; Assess)**

You learned the *pause* and how to identify your biases and help others identify theirs, the first step to *Breaking Free from Bias* for personal and organizational success.

You discovered additional options for identifying your biases.

What did you discover about your own bias from the Harvard Project Implicit Social Attitudes Assessment? https://implicit.harvard.edu/implicit/

Because we operate 98+% of the time from our unconscious, how do you become more conscious in order to identify your biases?

How are you inviting others to identify their biases?

What tools are you using to identify biases in your organization?

What biases are you identifying within your organization?

How might bias might be sabotaging your and your organization's success?

**Managing your bias (Help or Harm? Be Curious)**

Once you have identified your Bias (and helped others identify theirs):

How are you *Breaking Free from Biases* which are harming your organizational culture and thus impairing talent recruitment and retention, employee experience, organizational culture and adding to conflict?

What are you implementing to manage hiring and feedback bias?

How are you practicing and promoting respectful curiosity amongst different cultural as well as departmental groups within your organization?

What is the impact of practicing this step within your organization?

**Planning how to unleash untapped potential ________ (Marketing, Networking, Advocacy)**

You went on an organizational treasure hunt analysis, looking at who your organization is attracting (recruitment, extending to the board level) and promoting and how that was occurring, including networking, marketing, and advocacy.

You looked at what was helping and harming and how out of the box strategies could result in not only less bias but a more diverse workplace, offering fresh perspectives and innovations, with greater opportunity for reaching potential.

What have you discovered through your analysis as you consider:

- What is the make-up of your board?

- Who makes up the leadership team?
- Who are your recent hires?
- Where and how are you seeking new talent?
- Who is leaving your organization? (talent loss) Why? What is your process for discovering why?
- What is your organization's face to the world? (Who is featured in your marketing, media images?)

Who have you shared your findings with?

What are you implementing?

What results are you and your organization experiencing?

How will you continue to capitalize on these results?

At what intervals will you repeat your analysis?

**Acting on your strategic plan with awareness and accountability**

You discovered increased awareness and accountability supports *breaking free from bias* to fulfill individual and organizational potential, resulting in decreased conflict as well as improved talent recruitment and retention.

How are you implementing increased awareness of bias by asking others for feedback?

How are you sharing your awareness of others' bias through feedback?

How do you handle challenging conversations?

How are you building in accountability for bias in your strategic plan?

How are you holding yourself accountable?

How are you holding others accountable?

**Confidently communicating about bias to reduce costly conflict**

You learned how Google and others are communicating about bias to reduce costly conflict as well as how to get buy-in from your leadership team, with an ACHE approach.

How are you implementing ACHE (Awareness, Curiosity, Humility, Empathy)?

What are you listening for to raise awareness of bias?

How are you communicating with others regarding their bias?

How are you getting organizational buy-in from the leadership team for *Breaking Free from Bias* programs and coaching?

How are you taking cultural communication differences into account?

**Taking Stock of Your success and Repeat What is Working Well!**

Note: this is not a one-time activity, but one you will want to continue to return to. I invite you to schedule your IMPACT *Breaking Free from Bias* review at least once a quarter.

Congratulations on taking all six steps toward greater IMPACT, resulting in improved culture, talent recruitment and retention, reduced conflict, and resulting in everyone (including you) achieving their potential and contributing to organizational success. You are part of the solution.

In our final chapter, we will look at how to move forward through courage, persistence, and partnership.

## *IMPACT Questions*

How is your *Breaking Free from Bias* Scorecard now compared to where it was when you started reading this book?

What is working well that you will continue?

Where do you and your organization need to continue to develop?

How will you do that?

How often will you repeat this review process?

# CHAPTER 9 - MOVING FORWARD THROUGH COURAGE, PERSISTENCE, PARTNERSHIP

You began this book because you are a change maker. Change making takes courage, persistence, and partnership. You want to help create positive change within your organization through the IMPACT model of identifying and managing bias. You want to see everyone in the organization as well as the organization itself live up to their full potential. You care about the people you work with and are invested in their success as well as the organization's.

You realize the time for change is urgently now. You are beginning to identify bias at work, recognize its harmful effects and how crucial it is for you to know how to manage it for your career success. You are learning how to enter into courageous conversations to create this change within your organization. And you know, especially in small to mid-size organizations, that this can be a lonely, at times discouraging, journey. And it never ends! This work requires persistence.

What if any level or part of your organization still does not want to see that bias is blocking individual and therefore organizational potential, and possibly are even blaming lackluster organizational performance on people with different cultural norms, as we saw with criticism of Misaki and Ana?

For example, what if the executive team of John's organization continued to criticize and question his diverse hiring practices as well as his hires' behavior as well as blocking their promotions? John could *partner* with other leaders, including human resources, to have the challenging, courageous conversations around buy-in covered in Chapter 7 as well as ways of identifying bias from Chapter 3. External partners can provide further resources and support on this ongoing journey.

Without a holistic approach, efforts may be stalled out or thwarted at any level or by any group. For example, if expectations of managing a diverse workforce are not clear prerequisites for advancement, middle managers may be disinterested. *Breaking free from bias* is not a one-time training session. It needs to be integrated into existing training, policies and procedures. An effort to listen to all voices in setting the strategic plan and vision results in a sustainable organization. And it is driven and exemplified by those at the top level of leadership.

You read some examples of my partnering with human resource and other leadership team members so you understand how much easier it can be with an external partner. You can claim these same results within your organization with the training and support of my *Breaking Free from Bias* program and with my further assistance as an external coach.

*Breaking Free from Bias* for the IMPACT you desire. You can be part of the solution. It is worth it!

### *IMPACT Question*

How could you and your organization be even more successful in reaching your full potential, increasing your impact while decreasing costly conflict through getting the support you need?

# CONCLUSION

Congratulations on your progress in your *Breaking Free from Bias* journey. You have learned and are beginning to implement the Six Step Coaching IMPACT Process to *break free from bias.* You are starting to see some positive IMPACT in reduced conflict, improved workplace culture and employee experience, with enhanced talent recruitment and retention. This all boosts the bottom line. You and your colleagues experience a more inclusive, thriving organization where *unconscious bias* is not being denied or forced underground in shame. Rather *unconscious bias* is humbly acknowledged, assumptions updated and intentional decisions and interactions rule. You are feeling less overwhelmed, and more secure in your position. Moving forward, you are aware of additional resources which could further increase your IMPACT.

You might have been surprised to discover in the introduction that what can overwhelm and eat up much of your time often stems from the root cause of *unconscious bias.* This includes conflict, complaints, impaired culture and employee experience and engagement and resulting in talent loss. The result is limited opportunities within and for your organization. Even though you may consider yourself and your organization multi-culturally aware, you came to realize no one is judgment-free. We all have *unconscious bias.*

The statistics showed how critical and timely bias is related to organizational success. You learned from Pat's organization's example of how *unconscious bias* caused Misaki's career to stall out, which negatively impacted their organization's reputation and bottom line. You came to realize that applying my six step IMPACT process can create a thriving workforce and organization, making your job easier and more secure.

Chapter 1 revealed that what you do not know *may* hurt you, your coworkers and your organization. You came to see bias as an interference in Gallwey's "Potential=Performance-Interference" equation. You recognized this in my client David's potential being limited by his own bias. I invited to you to pause and consider your own bias experience. I shared with you some of my own pain related to bias which eventually led to the development of this book and my *Breaking Free from Bias* program. You welcomed this book and six step process as a simplified, immediately actionable path to *Breaking Free from Bias* for greater IMPACT.

How *unconscious bias* can play into hiring and promotion, rippling out to conflict, culture, talent recruitment and retention, and the employee experience, and affecting the bottom line was revisited in Chapter 2 with a hiring example from Pat's organization. You are learning more about *unconscious bias* and how little time we spend in our conscious. The six IMPACT steps are starting to make sense and sound doable.

You learned how to move through the blindness of *unconscious bias* to clearly identify it through three methods in Chapter 3, starting with the free Harvard assessment. Then you practiced my own quick *Bias Pause* with your scenario from Chapter 1. You were offered additional ways to identify bias that involve listening to the different voices in your organization. I shared with you how identifying and breaking free from an early *unconscious bias* was a key to a later business success for me. And how applying this step with my client Pat's leadership team led to greater trust and results.

Once you have identified bias, how do you learn to manage it so it does not manage you? In Chapter 4 we looked at examples of how stretching with curiosity through getting to know people of different cultural identities can help. Examples given included hiring scenarios and change in practice, getting to know people who hang out in bars, interviewing for a White Privilege Group, and a *My land, Your Land* activity. How will you spend more time with people who are different from you and promote this within your organization?

In Chapter 5 you learned how to access untapped potential. I offered questions to help you get a clear picture of the cultural identities that you and your organization are recruiting, retaining, and promoting. What might you be missing? With Google, Pat's advocacy and my example you learned how to retrieve and leverage buried treasure as well as how to fish in new ponds for new talent.

"How will you build accountability and awareness to ensure sustainable organizational success as you implement these IMPACT steps?" was the question at the end of Chapter 6. Through the application of awareness and accountability evidenced in the examples Ana and John; and Jane, you learned the importance of this step.

Chapter 7 emphasized the importance of ACHE in intercultural communication, which is *all* communication when you consider all our cultural identities. You discovered what to listen for that hints of bias and learned Randy's exercise for confronting it. You also learned to consider cultural differences that include how communication, including nonverbal, is given and received. How to communicate the organizational case for a bias initiative was also addressed.

You were invited to go through the *Breaking Free from Bias* Scorecard for a second time in Chapter 8. How is your *Breaking Free from Bias* Scorecard now compared to where it was when you started reading this book? What is working well that you will continue? How often will you repeat this review process?

In Chapter 9, you discovered how to move forward on this ongoing journey through courage, persistence, and partnership; using a holistic approach.

I have envisioned you as a bias hero, or even better, a member of the bias hero team, in your workplace: *Breaking Free from Bias* for your own good (your career and as a human being), for the good of others, and for the good of the organization. You can be part of the solution, a shining light. I look forward to our continued contact.

# FURTHER READING

*Blindspot* by Mahzarin R. Banaji, Anthony G. Greenwald, Bantam Books

*Blindspot* provides the science behind the IAT, Harvard's Implicit Bias Test. The IAT is one way of identifying bias, addressed in Chapter 3. The link to the free assessment is in Chapter 3 as well as the Breaking Free from Bias Toolkit available at https://marilynoh.com/breaking-free-from-bias.

*Presence Based Coaching* by Doug Silsbee, Jossey-Bass, a Wiley Imprint

This book addresses the importance of presence, particularly a centered presence in our VUCA (volatile, uncertain, complex and ambiguous) world. As referenced in Chapter 3, I learned the centering pause from Doug. You read about the benefits of this practice in multiple sections. Centering is related to mindfulness and can be incorporated into spiritual practices such as prayer and meditation. It is one way to bridge the gap between the unconscious and the conscious.

*Systemic Coaching & Constellations* by John Whittington, KoganPage

Another tool mentioned in Chapter 3 for identifying bias, systemic work is holistic and quickly gets to the roots of issues for teams and entire organizations.

Because this is a fairly new field, much of the available material is in articles rather than books.

For links to articles researched for this book, go to https://marilynoh.com/breaking-free-from-bias, sign up for the Breaking Free from Bias Programs and Opportunities list, and receive the Reference Links as part of the Toolkit.

# ADDITIONAL RESOURCES

***"Make use of available resources–you do not have to go it alone."***

–Marilyn O'Hearne

## Thank You

Congratulations! You are compassionately *Breaking Free from Bias!* You know how messy it can get, and you choose to do it anyway. Or you were chosen to do so anyway. I see you as a hero in this regard. You are aware of the painful barriers bias creates and are committed to *Breaking Free from those Biases,* for everyone's success, including your own. You have made it through all six steps, and now understand this is an ongoing process. There is no arrival point where we are totally free from bias.

And you know how important it is to have the internal and external support you need to be courageous and compassionate with *Breaking Free from Bias.* I invite you to consider me a coaching and program resource you can access. You do not have to go it alone. I am here for you. Like Ana, Amelia, David, Jane, John, Misaki and Pat, who you have read about.

**Still have some questions or want to connect with me further?**

I invite you to:

1. Sign up for your free Toolkit: Bias Pause Handout plus Reference Links at https://marilynoh.com/breaking-free-from-bias

2. Connect with me on Social Media:

    www.linkedin.com/in/marilynohearne

    www.facebook.com/CoachMarilynOh

3. Schedule a Strategy session with me at https://marilynoh.com/breaking-free-from-bias

4. Post on social media your successes with IMPACT Bias Breakthroughs! I want to hear about it! Sensitive information? Email me: marilyn@marilynoh.com

I look forward to staying connected with you and supporting you in your *Breaking Free from Bias!*

# BREAKING FREE FROM BIAS SCORECARD

You are invited to use this scorecard both before and after reading and implementing the six IMPACT steps to *Breaking Free from Bias.* Then compare the two to reveal your progress as well as areas for further development.

## 1. Identifying your biases (Pause; Assess)

What did you discover about your own bias from the Harvard Project Implicit Social Attitudes Assessment?

– https://implicit.harvard.edu/implicit/

1. Before:
2. After:

Because we operate 98+% of the time from our unconscious, how do you become more conscious in order to identify your biases?

1. Before:
2. After:

How are you inviting others to identify their biases?

1. Before:
2. After:

What tools are you using to identify biases in your organization?

1. Before:
2. After:

What biases have you identified within your organization?

1. Before:
2. After:

How might bias be sabotaging your and your organization's success?

1. Before:
2. After:

## 2. Managing your bias (Help or Harm? Be Curious)

Once you have identified your bias (and helped others identify theirs):

How are you *Breaking Free from Biases* which are harming your organizational culture and thus impairing talent recruitment and retention, employee experience, organizational culture and adding to conflict?

1. Before:
2. After:

What are you implementing to manage hiring and feedback bias?

1. Before:
2. After:

How are you practicing and promoting respectful curiosity amongst different cultural as well as departmental groups within your organization?

1. Before:
2. After:

What is the impact of practicing this step within your organization?

1. Before:
2. After:

### 3. Planning how to unleash untapped potential (Marketing, Networking, Advocacy)

In Chapter Five you go on an organizational treasure hunt analysis, looking at who your organization is attracting (recruitment, extending to the board level) and promoting and how that occurs, including networking, marketing, and advocacy.

You look at what helps and harms and how out of the box strategies could result in not only less bias but a more diverse workplace, offering fresh perspectives and innovations, with greater opportunity for reaching potential.

What do you discover through your analysis as you consider:

What is the make-up of your board?

1. Before:
2. After:

Who makes up the leadership team?

1. Before:
2. After:

Who are your recent hires?

1. Before:
2. After:

Where and how are you seeking new talent?

1. Before:
2. After:

Who is leaving your organization? (talent loss) Why? What is your process for discovering why?

1. Before:
2. After:

What is your organization's face to the world? (Who is featured in your marketing, media images?)

1. Before:
2. After:

Who are you sharing your findings with?

1. Before:
2. After:

What are you implementing?

1. Before:
2. After:

What results are you and your organization experiencing?

1. Before:
2. After:

How will you continue to capitalize on these results?

1. Before:
2. After:

At what intervals will you repeat your analysis?

1. Before:
2. After:

## 4. Acting on your strategic plan with awareness and accountability

You discover increased awareness and accountability supports *breaking free from bias* to fulfill individual and organizational potential, resulting in decreased conflict as well as improved talent recruitment and retention.

How are you implementing increased awareness of bias by asking others for feedback?

1. Before:
2. After:

How are you sharing your awareness of others' bias through feedback?

1. Before:
2. After:

How do you handle challenging conversations?

1. Before:
2. After:

How are you building in accountability for bias in your strategic plan?

1. Before:
2. After:

How are you holding yourself accountable?

1. Before:
2. After:

How are you holding others accountable?

1. Before:
2. After:

## 5. Confidently communicating about bias to reduce costly conflict

You learn how Google and others are communicating about bias to reduce costly conflict as well as how to get buy-in from your leadership team; with an ACHE approach.

How are you implementing ACHE (Awareness, Curiosity, Humility, Empathy)?

1. Before:
2. After:

What are you listening for to raise awareness of bias?

1. Before:
2. After:

How are you communicating with others regarding their bias?

1. Before:
2. After:

How are you getting organizational buy-in from the leadership team for *Breaking Free from Bias* programs and coaching?

1. Before:
2. After:

How are you taking cultural communication differences into account?

1. Before:
2. After:

## 6. Taking Stock of Your success and Repeat What is Working Well!

What is working well?

1. Before:
2. After:

What areas need further development?

1. Before:
2. After:

How will you do that?

1. Before:
2. After:

How often will you repeat this review process?

1. Before:
2. After:

Note: this is not a one time activity, but one you will want to continue to return to. I invite you to calendar your IMPACT *Breaking Free from Bias* review at least once a quarter.

You may also download this scorecard from:

https://marilynoh.com/breaking-free-from-bias-scorecard

# ACKNOWLEDGMENTS

With deep gratitude to my parents, John O'Hearne, MD and Lillian O'Hearne, MD, for taking me to the Russian physician's meeting, my first *Breaking Free from Bias* experience. And for taking our family across town, past the racial dividing line, to have dinner with an African American family. I will never forget the barbed wire fence and their fierce German Shepard to protect their property. At that time, I was shocked to discover they were limited to where they could live not by income but by race. And thanks to my parents for hosting an interracial wedding in our home because it was on the state of Kansas side of Kansas City and legal, vs. the state of Missouri where interracial marriage was not yet legal. These powerful childhood experiences triggered my "that's not fair!" indignation. Now I have been called to do something about it-to write this book to help identify and manage bias, to limit its harmful effects, to contribute towards a world of peace and shared power, my vision.

Mom also told all four of us, "You can be whoever you choose to be," and she modeled that, becoming one of three women in her medical school class to earn their license, despite being asked during her interview if she were just there to meet a husband. She actually turned down several marriage proposals because she did not want marriage to interfere with completing her training. She broke free from bias to achieve her accomplishments.

Dad, despite being raised in the segregated South of the U.S., was on staff at both the Christian and Jewish hospitals at a time when this was uncommon. He burst bias barriers when brought to Kansas City to establish the first Mental Health Center, insisted that it be one for all, rather than separate, one for whites and one for "coloreds" as the General Hospital was at that time.

My parents also served as role models in welcoming different cultural groups to our home which prevented biases from forming: singles, divorced and widowed, Jews and Christians, their secretary from Mexico and friend from Japan, including our open table holiday meals. They took their Mexican colleague's offer to host us in their home seriously, and sent me by myself to Mexico City at my request the summer I turned 16 to learn more of the language and culture. They have been lifelong learners, including of languages and cultures.

Our primary dinner topic was people. In this sense and no doubt many other ways I followed in my parents' footsteps, reading all the orange cloth covered biographies in the school library as a child. My studies followed this focus on people and culture, with my BA in Social Sciences: Psychology, Cultural Anthropology and Sociology, including a semester in Spain, with post graduate work at the Intercultural Communication Institute and Systems Theory, and teaching Organizational

Behavior and International Business in Hong Kong and Malaysia.

My daughters Amelia and Claire continue the tradition of service as well as learning about cultures through their careers as teacher and Pastor. Amelia was on staff with an International School in Korea for three years, just as their dad and I had worked in Brazil for two years.

I have also learned a great deal about bias through readings as well as my work with my leadership coaching clients and human resources partners. I have had my own awareness stretched by my colleagues on the International Coach Federation Global Board of Directors as well as the Association of Coach Training Organization and the White Privilege Faculty. Patti Digh's Hard Conversations About Racism course also contributed, as did my participation in my students' Coaching for Social Action course. And Doug Silsbee's centering exercise led to my fleshing out my *pause* in a neuroscience frame of reference.

I give thanks for colleagues who shared resources, challenged my comments and thinking as well as supporting me through the pain of bias and making this journey less lonely and discouraging. I appreciate those who have encouraged and supported my writing starting in grade school as well as those who contributed to this book through editing, interviewing, early reading, Advance Praise, permission to use quotes, and support. Acknowledgment is one of my daily practices, personally and professionally. I hope all of you who have contributed to this book experience my deep gratitude.

Last but certainly not least thanks to you, readers, who pushed past any initial, "Bias, not me!" reactions to courageously dig in and experiment with the Six Step Coaching IMPACT *Breaking Free from Bias* process: **I**dentify, **M**anage, **P**lan, increase your **A**wareness and **A**ccountability, improve your intercultural **C**ommunication (because all our work is intercultural) and **T**ake stock and repeat your successes. You are my heroes, acting out of service to your co-workers and your organization, without fearing that their success may cause you to lose some of yours. In fact, you are contributing to decreased conflict, threat of lawsuits, complaints, improved culture, talent recruitment and retention, and employee experience, which boosts the bottom line and therefore enhances your career.

I appreciate the opportunity to be your partner on this part of your journey through this book.

# ABOUT THE AUTHOR

Marilyn O'Hearne, MA, International Coach Federation Master Certified Coach, is the founder of Breaking Free from Bias programs. She has been helping leaders and coaches achieve breakthrough results since 1998, in 28 countries. She is known for her United Nations Leadership Development Coaching. Her clients move from the overwhelming uncertainty of our rapidly changing world to clarity, focus and confidence. Marilyn has been described as a "gentle, spiritual soul, and yet powerful and provocative at the same time," by a program participant.

"It is impossible to not work interculturally!" Marilyn says, understanding the painful consequences of conflict and business losses due to lack of Cultural Intelligence and *unconscious bias.*

With this awareness, Marilyn invests in her clients, developing their abilities and visions and capitalizing on those. This leads to not only the avoidance of burnout and loss of talent but also the contribution of Quadruple Bottom Line results (People, Profit, Planet, Purpose), reflecting her strong belief in stewardship.

Marilyn's experience includes Adjunct Professor of Organizational Behavior and International Business in Hong Kong and Malaysia and living in Brazil and Spain. A leader herself, Marilyn served as Director of Education for a nonprofit in Brazil as well as six years as Director, Global Boards for the International Coach Federation and two years for the Association of Coach Training Organizations.

Marilyn's numerous articles include columns in *The Kansas City Star* newspaper and in *The Brazil Herald/Latin American Daily Post,* and contributions to two books, including *Professional Ethics and Legal Issues in Coaching (The Intersection of Culture and Ethics);*. She is much in demand by and is quoted by media sources, and a popular global speaker.

Awards include the 2015 Thomas Leonard Achievement Award: Honoring Vision and Innovation.

**Website:** www.marilynoh.com

**Email:** marilyn@marilynoh.com

**Facebook:** www.facebook.com/CoachMarilynOh

**LinkedIn:** www.linkedin.com/in/marilynohearne